HOW DO Y

KNOW WHEN

YOU'RE REALLY IN

love?

AN LDS GUIDE TO DATING, COURTSHIP, AND MARRIAGE

ROBERT K. McINTOSH

BOOKCRAFT

SALT LAKE CITY, UTAH

Library of Congress Cataloging-in-Publication Data

McIntosh, Robert K., 1942–
    How do you know when you're really in love? / Robert K. McIntosh.
      p.   cm.
    Includes bibliographical references.
    ISBN 978-1-57345-647-0 (pbk.)
    1. Marriage—Religious aspects—Church of Jesus Christ of Latter-day Saints.   2. Love—Religious aspects—Church of Jesus Christ of Latter-day Saints.   3. Young adults—Religious life. I. Title.

BX8641 .M39 2000
248.4'89332—dc21   00-021325

Printed in the United States of America
R. R. Donnelley and Sons, Allentown, PA

20 19 18 17 16 15 14

To Susan's and my grandchildren—those born and those yet unborn:

Robert, Kacie, Madison, and Morgan McIntosh
Kennedy, Connor, Aidan, Fiona, and Bridgett McIntosh
Brittany Ware
Tyler, Alexander, and Paris Lukes
Austin Jordan, Baylee, and Carter Boden
Brooklyn, Christian, and Chole McIntosh

You are the joy and the light of our lives. Our greatest hope and prayer is that in eternity there will be no "empty chairs."

Contents

Section 4: Choosing for Eternity

Acknowledgments

Most books are the results of the efforts, not just of the author, but of many people. This is certainly the case with this book. I would like to sincerely thank the following:

Prophets and Church leaders, past and present, for their inspiration, guidance, and example relative to the principles in this book. I hope I have represented well their teachings.

Shirley R. Klein, Dale E. LeBaron, Howard Hamilton, Douglas E. Brinley, William O. Nelson, and Lee Benson, for their careful review, insights, and editing of the manuscript.

Leonard Tourney, who acted as a sounding board and adviser for many of the ideas in this book.

Frederick G. Williams, for helping me understand the nature of godly love, through discussions and through his example.

Cory Maxwell and staff, for having faith and confidence that this book might make a difference in the lives of young people.

Richard Peterson, for his skillful edit of the manuscript.

Nanci Gardiner, for typing the manuscript and for her constant encouragement.

The Church Educational System, for allowing me to serve some of the finest youth in the Church.

My many students and friends of the past thirty years. Thank you for all you have taught me and for the example you have been of the teachings of Jesus Christ.

Our children, their companions, and our wonderful grandchildren. From you I have learned a dimension of love that has blessed my life eternally.

Susan, for being my friend, eternal companion, and example of all that is good in this book. Thank you for loving me.

Finally, I take full responsibility for the errors and omissions in this book. All that is good is the result of the contributions of those I have mentioned.

Introduction

To attempt to define and understand love is a most challenging task! A song from my youth acknowledges the difficulty by asking, "Who can explain it, who can tell you why?" And concluding, "Fools give you reasons, wise men never try."[1]

And yet love is vital to our lives and to the gospel of Jesus Christ, for the scriptures teach that "God is love" (1 John 4:8). So it must be possible to gain some understanding of this wonderful phenomenon, which philosophers, religious leaders, writers, and poets have grappled with since time began. Sometimes they have diagrammed stages of love, and other times they have drawn comparisons showing what love is and what it isn't. One thing is certain: there are many dimensions to love. Like a diamond, it is multifaceted and not just one thing.

One Latter-day Saint leader, Elder Joe J. Christensen of the First Quorum of the Seventy, borrowed from the Greek lexicon to describe three dimensions of love. In his insightful discussion of this subject, Elder Christensen says one Greek word for love is *eros*, which suggests romantic love. This is the kind of love that exists between a man and a woman. It involves the affectionate feelings that initially attract two people to each other and which are so vital in courtship and in the strengthening of marital bonds. The English word *erotic* comes from that Greek root.

The second category of love is *philia*. The emotions involved here are those we are capable of feeling for our parents, siblings, relatives, friends, neighbors, and associates. It is to this the Lord referred when he commanded us to love our neighbors. Philadelphia, which calls itself the "City of Brotherly Love," derives its name from this Greek root.

Finally, the Greeks differentiated a third type of love—*agape*. This is godlike love, of the type manifested in Deity's capacity to love us in spite of our deficiencies. This is the word used in the Greek text of the New Testament each time the Lord commands us to love our enemies. It is also the type of love that allows us to overlook our companion's faults or shortcomings and to freely forgive offenses. [2]

Some people have construed these three dimensions of love as stages, one rising to another. To do so makes one dimension of love appear to be more important than another. In my experience, a broader view of love takes into consideration all three of these dimensions, although there may be times when one aspect is stressed more than another in our lives. For example, the romantic nature of love is clearly more dominant in the period of courtship, but it should remain an integral part of the relationship throughout the marriage.

Living the gospel provides an analogy of how these three aspects of love are related. A gospel-centered life is one where our physical, social, intellectual, emotional, and spiritual dimensions are all integrated. So it is with love. Love encompasses the physical, social, intellectual, emotional, and spiritual aspects of our lives. Using Elder Christensen's description of love, romantic love would be the physical aspect; friendship love would include the social, intellectual, and emotional aspects; and Christlike love would involve the spiritual. A diagram of love that encompasses all three dimensions looks like this:

In this book I will attempt, with the help and guidance of the standard works and the teachings of Church leaders, to describe each of these dimensions of love. In doing so, I will not attempt to interpret doctrine, for that is the province of the First Presidency of the Church. We will also examine Satan's half-truths about love, in an effort to expose his tactics as he labors to make us as miserable as he is. I will also discuss the importance of preparing for a celestial marriage so that you can be worthy of and attract the type of person that you will love forever. We will look closely at how we properly go about choosing a marriage partner, bearing in mind the enormous importance of the temple in this regard. One of the most important questions we will explore is "Am I in love enough to marry?" By this I mean are you in love enough to accept all of the demands of married life—financial, physical, emotional, and spiritual?

At the conclusion of each chapter is a list of assignments that will assist you to apply the principles and ideas you have read. Much of what you receive from this book will be the result of completing these assignments and pondering the questions that are posed.

Everything we know about our Heavenly Father's plan for us suggests that he wants us to have a happy, joyous marriage—both here in mortality and throughout eternity. To assist you in your pursuit of this great blessing is the purpose of this book.

Marriage
IS ORDAINED OF GOD

"When two Latter-day Saints are united together in marriage, promises are made to them concerning their offspring that reach from eternity to eternity. They are promised that they shall have the power and the right to govern and control and administer salvation and exaltation and glory to their offspring worlds without end. And what offspring they do not have here, undoubtedly there will be opportunities to have them hereafter. What else could man wish? A man and a woman in the other life, having celestial bodies, free from sickness and disease, glorified and beautified beyond description, standing in the midst of their posterity, governing and controlling them, administering life, exaltation and glory worlds without end!" (Lorenzo Snow, as quoted by Spencer W. Kimball, *Ensign*, October 1979, 6).

CHAPTER 1

What Kind of Marriage Do You Want?

❧

*"We the First Presidency and Council of the Twelve
Apostles of The Church of Jesus Christ of
Latter-day Saints, solemnly proclaim that marriage
between a man and a woman is ordained of God
and that the family is central to the Creator's plan
for the destiny of His children"* (The Family:
A Proclamation to the World).

❧

For over thirty years I have had the privilege of teaching, counseling, and listening to the concerns of young people. Most of the questions I have been asked can be grouped under two headings: 1) concerns about testimony or worthiness and 2) questions about relationships. One of the most frequently asked questions regarding relationships has been "How will I know when I'm really in love?"

This is an especially important consideration if you are in a serious relationship now or plan to be so in the future. Each time I have been asked this question, I have felt somewhat overwhelmed and inadequate to respond. After over thirty years of marriage, I know how important the answer to that question has been to me. It has not only affected my happiness here but will dictate where I will spend eternity! The answer to this question has also affected the children my wife and I have brought into this world. Their happiness and well-being has been directly related to the decision I made many years ago about whom to marry. Of such decisions, Elder Bruce R. McConkie has said: "The most important things that any member of The

Church of Jesus Christ of Latter-day Saints ever does in this world are: 1) To marry the right person, in the right place, by the right authority; and 2) To keep the covenant made in connection with this holy and perfect order of matrimony—thus assuring the obedient persons of an inheritance of exaltation in the celestial kingdom."[1]

It is one of the ironies of life that the season in which we are making such far-reaching and important decisions is while we are young, when we have not yet had the experiences that will enable us to act rationally and make sound judgments. Our ability to choose wisely is also sometimes impaired by our emotions and the passions that are so active in our youth and young-adult years. Given all the forces that are involved, it is not easy to define our feelings or to know what it is we are to do. Yet, as President Spencer W. Kimball has said, marriage "has to do not only with immediate happiness, but eternal joys as well. It affects not only the two people involved, but also their families and particularly their children and their children's children down through the many generations."[2] That sobering statement reminds us of how important it is to marry wisely and well. You'll not make a more important or far-reaching decision in your life.

Here are some reasons young people like you have shared with me regarding why they feel the marriage decision is so important:

- Our eternal happiness hinges on this decision.
- We will spend more time with the person we marry than with anyone else.
- We will share with this person our greatest intimacies, innermost thoughts, hopes, and fears.
- Together we will bring children into this world, and our marriage relationship and the home we provide will have a profound effect on their happiness and stability.
- We will share life's most significant problems, successes, and failures with our marriage partner.
- We will likely grow old together.

Before answering the question "How will I know when I am really in love?" I ask my students to consider such things as: What types of people will I date? What will I do and not do on dates? What role will the gospel play in my preparation for marriage? What kind of marriage do I want? I ask them to picture in their minds the type of relationship they would like to have with their future companion. I then ask them to describe this relationship. Young people have given me such answers as:

- "The gospel will be central to our relationship. God will be our partner, and we will work to help each other become like Him."
- "We will totally trust each other and be open and accepting of one another."
- "We will have a deep friendship where we respect, forgive, and cherish each other."
- "We will have an equal partnership where all responsibilities are shared."
- "We will understand each other because we will listen to each other."
- " Our love will continue to grow and will not diminish with the years."

Once they have shared their picture of the kind of marriage they would like, I often ask, "What does the temple have to do with your picture of an ideal marriage?" Sometimes young people will see a direct correlation between the blessings of the temple and the qualities they want in their ideal marriage. Others have a difficult time seeing how the temple ordinances prepare them for a wonderful marriage. Some have said:

"I want to be married in the temple because ever since I was young it has been expected of me."

"The temple is the only place I can be married forever."

"I don't want to disappoint my parents."

"I will have a happier marriage if I'm married in the temple."

I have found that many young people have no idea how the temple can help them achieve the type of marriage they want. Some think that if they can just be married in the temple they will have no problems in marriage. Many couples have learned that this simply is not true. Elder LeGrand Richards told the story of a grandmother who told her grandson that now that he was getting married he was at the end of his problems. After six months of marriage the boy went to his grandmother and said, "Why did you tell me that when I got married I'd be at the end of my problems? I have more problems now than before my marriage!" The grandmother smiled and said, "When I told you that you would be at the end of your problems, I didn't mention which end!"[3]

We bring to marriage the sum total of who we are—our habits, attitudes, likes, and dislikes. Once we are married, we find that there are some adjustments that need to be made because of differences between our personality and that of our marriage partner. There are also tremendous stresses placed upon marriages by society. Bills must be paid, deadlines must be met, responsibilities must be fulfilled. Marriage is not a cure-all for problems! Elder Marion D. Hanks emphasized this when he said: "The sealing ceremony in the temple is to us beautiful and indispensable, but it does not automatically assure a successful marriage. Such a marriage is brought about, not by circumstance or chance, but by two mature, loving adults, who are able and willing to learn the principles upon which a genuine and durable marriage may be fashioned and who, day-by-day, year-by-year, earnestly make the effort, building on the solid foundation of the covenants of the temple."[4]

I have asked many young married couples the greatest lesson they have learned about making a marriage work. A typical answer would be: "We have learned that it takes effort and hard, hard work!" Because of this, you must consider seriously and carefully what kind of marriage you want and decide if you are willing to pay the price to achieve that type of marriage. Just as there are different degrees of glory in the life to come, marriages differ in their quality and degree of happiness. When I think about a happy, successful marriage, I like the term *celestial marriage* because it suggests a type or quality of marriage. You need to be aware, though, that it is possible to marry in the temple and yet not have a "celestial marriage." However, a "celestial marriage" can be achieved only through the ordinances provided in the house of the Lord.

The Lord is the best source of information on this topic, and he has revealed some important truths: "For, behold, the mystery of godliness, how great is it! For, behold, I am endless, and the punishment which is given from my hand is endless punishment, for Endless is my name. Wherefore—eternal punishment is God's punishment. Endless punishment is God's punishment" (D&C 19:10–12).

Here we learn that the words *Eternal* and *Endless* are God's names. Therefore, eternal punishment is God's punishment. Eternal life is God's life. Though the term *eternal* can be used to mean *forever*, it also refers to a type or quality of life: "God's life."

Applying this to marriage, we find that "eternal marriage is God's marriage." In other words, when we desire an eternal marriage, we want a type or quality of marriage that is godlike. Through the blessings of the temple, such a marriage will last forever because the couple is striving to build their relationship on the teachings of the Lord. An eternal marriage is therefore a celestial marriage. The very key to a celestial marriage is the keeping of our temple covenants. The following diagram contrasts three types of marriages:

MARRIAGE OUTSIDE THE TEMPLE	TEMPLE MARRIAGE	CELESTIAL MARRIAGE
Performed by someone authorized by man	Performed by someone authorized by the state and by God	Performed by someone authorized by the state and by God
Anyone may attend	Selected people may attend	Selected people may attend
	The couple make solemn covenants	The couple make solemn covenants
		The couple keep their covenants

As you look at this, you will see that though a couple may be married in the temple, they achieve a celestial marriage only by keeping their covenants.

In Doctrine and Covenants 131:2, celestial marriage is referred to as "the new and everlasting covenant of marriage." It is "new" because the principle and ordinance has been restored in our day. It is an "everlasting covenant" because the marriage has the potential to endure forever, if the partners keep the covenants they have made in the temple. Elder Marion D. Hanks emphasized the importance of these covenants when he said: "It is simple to see, isn't it, that the kind of marriage we are talking about doesn't just happen. Nobody can pronounce happiness. No one can pronounce the quality that forgives and thus expresses real love. These are the elements in lives that have to be brought to the union by those involved, grown in and developed in—through the course. The foundation can be laid in the House of the Lord. The marriage can be pronounced by the authority of God, but it must be fashioned by two who are wholesome, prepared emotionally and practically, and who are honest. It requires being *ready* to go to the temple, being mature enough to *make* and *keep* promises and to *receive* holy promises and *qualify* for their fulfillment."[5]

By kneeling at a sacred altar in the holy temple and entering into covenants, we bring the Lord into our marriage. He then can help us grow together and become one with him, thus helping us achieve the type of marriage we want. We have then formed a triangle of love, with our covenants serving as the binding force.

Elder Marlin K. Jensen shared an experience that illustrates the power of temple covenants in helping a marriage endure the trials of life and become a celestial union. He told of a visit he had with a man whose wife had just passed away. The man and his wife had been married for fifty-three years. During the last six years of their marriage, she had been seriously ill with a terminal kidney disease. The husband had provided the 24-hour care she required until his own health was affected. Elder Jensen asked the man how he had been able to give such love and care. The man replied that it had been easy because he had made a commitment fifty-three years earlier when he had knelt at an altar in the temple and made a covenant with the Lord and with his bride. "I wanted to keep that covenant," he said. Elder Jensen concluded the story by saying, "In an eternal marriage the thought of ending what began with a covenant between God and each other simply has little place. When challenges come and our individual weaknesses are revealed, the remedy is to repent, improve, and apologize, not to separate or divorce. When we make covenants with the Lord and our eternal companion, we should do everything in our power to honor the terms."[6] To achieve a celestial or eternal quality of marriage a couple must be willing to abide by the covenants the Lord has established. These covenants can be made only in the house of the Lord (see D&C 132:7). I call these the "covenants of exaltation." It is in keeping these covenants that we achieve the kind of marriage we want.

I have had young people ask me what I feel is the most important ingredient in a happy, eternal marriage. Almost without hesitation I have replied, "Commitment—the will to make it work." By this I mean two things:

First, a commitment to the Lord to do whatever he asks of us. With such a commitment we can overcome the challenges and problems faced in marriage.

Second, a commitment to each other and to the covenants of exaltation made at the altar of the temple. Commitment involves character. It means doing what you say you will do even when you do not feel like it. This type of commitment will help a couple weather almost any storm that can come in marriage: financial worries, concern over children, health problems, or personality differences. The Lord instructed Emma Smith, the wife of the Prophet Joseph Smith, to "cleave unto the covenants which thou hast made" (D&C 25:13). We cleave to our covenants by keeping the promises we have made.

Elder Spencer J. Condie of the First Quorum of the Seventy referred to these temple covenants as the "common bond" between husband and wife. "I have been disappointed with a number of couples who file for divorce contending that 'We have nothing in common.' There are, indeed, vast differences between men and women, regardless of any other background factors. However, once a couple have knelt across the sacred altar in a sealing room in the house of the Lord, they have the most important things of eternity in common, and this common bond can overcome all differences."[7]

The importance of this "common" commitment or bond was taught very forcibly to me on the day Susan and I were sealed in the temple. Elder LeGrand Richards of the Quorum of the Twelve performed our marriage ceremony. After saying some beautiful words to us, he had us kneel across from each other at the altar. This was to be the time of making a solemn covenant, a covenant that would bind us forever to each other. He pronounced the words clearly, and we made our covenant. He then had us stand side-by-side at the head of the altar and look into a set of mirrors that were hung facing each other on opposite walls. We could see our reflections in them, repeated endlessly. Elder Richards gave us a moment to gaze at the effect, then said to me, "Brother McIntosh, do you know what it means to have Susan for all eternity?" I paused and then gave the answer that I thought was correct, "We will be married forever."

Elder Richards shook his finger at me and said, "Can you fathom what *forever* means?" I shook my head in the negative. "Well, he said, I like to round it down to the nearest millionth, something I can comprehend. If you live worthily you will have Susan for 300 million years." He chuckled as he said so. *Three hundred million years*, I thought; *this covenant is surely important!*

Elder Richards taught me a great lesson at that time. The covenants we make with our eternal companion are not to be entered into lightly. Three hundred million years leaves little room for divorce. So, what kind of marriage do you want?

Assignment

Write a paragraph or two describing how you imagine your future marriage and family will be. As you do so, ask yourself the following questions:

- What place will the gospel of Jesus Christ have in my relationship with my spouse?

- What will the spiritual atmosphere be in my home?

- How will I relate to my spouse on a day-to-day basis?

- How do I imagine myself facing and resolving challenges and disappointments?

- Is going to the temple important to me? For what reasons?

CHAPTER 2

Marriage and Your Plan of Happiness

❧

"For behold, this is my work and my glory—
to bring to pass the immortality and eternal life
of man" (Moses 1:39).

❧

Have you ever stopped to consider that God's work and glory is to help you achieve happiness in this life and for all eternity? The Prophet Joseph Smith said, "Happiness is the object and design of our existence."[1] Much of the happiness you experience here and in eternity will depend on the type of marriage you have. Right now, by the decisions you are making, you are determining to a great degree how happy you will be in marriage.

You have probably already learned that a relationship gone sour results in great unhappiness and misery. After having had a sad experience in a relationship, many students have said to me, "My life is over! I'm so depressed! I never want to date again!!" If you have had such an experience, you have probably wondered, "If God wants me to be happy, why are relationships so challenging?"

In trying to answer that difficult question, I think of what the Lord taught Joseph Smith while the Prophet was confined in Liberty Jail. Referring to the physical hardships, the anxiety Joseph experienced in behalf of his family, and the mental duress Joseph had endured over many months, the Lord said to Joseph: "All these things shall give thee experience, and shall be for thy good" (D&C 122:7).

God's plan gives us the precious gift of choice. We have that gift and so do others. With choice, come consequences. Often, we do not want to accept the consequences of our choices, nor do we want others to make choices that affect our happiness. However, that is not the way it is in life nor is it the way God, our Father, meant it to be. When young people come to me, having lost someone they have felt was their one and only true love, I often have them read what the Lord told Joseph. Then I ask them, "What have you learned from this relationship that will help you in later relationships?" I have tried to help my students understand that part of God's plan for us here in mortality is to gain experience and to grow and to mature therefrom. The fact is, sometimes relationships reach a dead end, and one or the other decides it's time to make a change. If you are rejected, you can roll up in a ball and feel sorry for yourself, or you can square your shoulders and ask, "What can I learn from this experience that will be of benefit later on?"

Unhappiness in a relationship can often be traced to immorality. A young man and a young woman who compromise their values to indulge in inappropriate intimate behavior often attempt to justify what they are doing by insisting they are in love or are only expressing their affection for each other. But what Alma told his son Corianton so long ago remains true: "Wickedness never was happiness" (Alma 41:10), and far from enhancing a relationship, immoral behavior introduces stress and feelings of guilt that destroy mutual respect and create discord. The Prophet Joseph Smith taught that "happiness is the object and design of our existence; and will be the end thereof, *if we pursue the path that leads to it*; and this path is virtue, uprightness, faithfulness, holiness, and keeping all the commandments of God"[2]

You must also ever remember that there is one who has another plan for you. He is called the adversary, and he is opposed to everything good and wonderful that the Lord has in store for you. His aim is to turn your life upside down, for he desires that you "might be miserable like unto himself" (2 Nephi 2:27). He has real power, and you must be aware of his plan and the strategies he employs to lead you away from the path of happiness. The Lord told the Prophet Joseph Smith, "Satan thinketh to overpower your testimony" (D&C 10:33).

I have known many young people who have allowed Satan to

overpower them and lead them along the paths of unhappiness. This usually begins in the teenage years, when parents and Church leaders may seem old-fashioned and out-of-date in comparison to friends and whatever fads or trends are being promoted by the media and attractive public personalities. Habits and thought patterns entered into in a spirit of experimentation can be just as binding as those willfully adopted, and if you are not careful, your friends can lead you into habits that will be extremely difficult to break later on. Sin is never easy to overcome; it requires effort, sincere repentance, and the help of the Lord.

I once learned a valuable lesson from one of my students, a handsome young man who had left the gospel path at about the age of fourteen. He became involved with his friends in the immorality and drug scene of his day and got to the point where he no longer believed in God, let alone the Church. After five years of living such a life, he came to the realization that true, lasting happiness is not to be found in the way of life he was following. He opened the scriptures and began to reexamine the faith in which he had been raised. He came to understand that the gospel of Jesus Christ is the plan that leads to happiness in this life and eternal life in the world to come. The Spirit of the Lord began to guide and direct the decisions he was making. His faith in Jesus Christ and his atoning sacrifice began to grow, and he desired to change his ways through the gift of repentance. Soon he went to his bishop and began the repentance process. He became an outstanding leader in our institute and helped a number of other young people find their way back to the Lord.

One day I was visiting with him and asked how he had been able to change after living for five years in sin and transgression.

He replied, "When I became involved in the gospel again, I found peace and happiness that I had never known before. I decided I never wanted to go back to my old way of life. So I developed my own plan for happiness."

"Your own plan for happiness?" I asked.

"Yes," he said, "I decided that if I wanted to be married in the temple and have an eternal family, I needed to set some goals that would ensure my receiving those great blessings. I made two lists, of

Don'ts and Do's. I placed this list by my bed, where I could see it every day, and it has been a constant guide to me ever since."

He then showed me some of the Don'ts and Do's he had written.

Don'ts
I will not drink alcohol.
I will not use drugs.
I will not have premarital sex.
I will not date anyone who does not have high standards and ideals.
I will not view or listen to any pornographic or sexually suggestive material.

Do's
I will live worthy of the Holy Spirit and follow its promptings.
I will study the scriptures on a daily basis.
I will say my prayers at least night and morning.
I will attend church services every Sunday.

President Spencer W. Kimball has counseled youth to do the very thing this young man did: "Our young people should drive down stakes early, indicating their paths. The stakes are of two kinds: 'This I will do' and 'This I will not do.' These decisions pertain to general activities, standards, spiritual goals, and personal programs. They should include anticipations for marriage and family. Very early, youth should have been living by a plan. . . . When such a course is charted and the goal is set, it is easier to resist the many temptations and to say 'no' to the first cigarette, 'no' to the first drink, 'no' to the car ride which will take one to the dark, lonely and hazardous places, 'no' to the first improper advances which lead eventually to immoral practices."[3]

Do you see the wisdom in deciding long before the temptation comes what you will and will not do? What problems could you have avoided in the past had you done this? Such a practice can help ensure that you achieve a celestial marriage.

Assignment

1. Consider carefully these questions: "If I continue on the path I am on right now, where will I end up?" "What type of marriage and family will I have?"

2. To help you achieve the type of marriage and family you desire, take a sheet of paper and write down your own plan for happiness: "This I will do." "This I will not do."

CHAPTER 3

Six Popular Marriage Myths

❦

"Take heed that no man deceive you"
(*JS—Matthew 1:5*).

❦

The world you live in, as you know, is very challenging. There are so many different philosophies about marriage and how to select a mate that some people are understandably confused. These myths are perpetuated and become part of our culture so that even some members of the Church have false ideas about love and marriage. Here are six common myths you need to be aware of.

Myth 1: We chose a marriage partner before we were born.

Some young people spend their dating years looking for the one person they chose in premortality—their so-called "soul mate." They believe that when they meet this person there will be an immediate attraction because they have already selected each other. Such young people believe that marriages were made in heaven. Consider an experience Brother Truman Madsen once had with President and Sister Joseph Fielding Smith.

"I was in the Church offices when I ran into his wife. Since she was going into his office, she took me with her. 'Let's go see Daddy,' she said. I knew who Daddy was. As the great Church scripturalist, he overawed me. He looked up with a smile and said, 'Brother Madsen, you can have one question.' So I asked, 'Brother Smith, do you think marriages are made in heaven?' Well, I had him over a barrel—his wife was standing right there. And he hesitated, so she kind of punched him. 'Daddy, Daddy, don't you think our marriage was made in heaven?' Now, he had to be honest. So he said, 'Well, it's in heaven now.'"[1]

Here is what Joseph Fielding Smith taught publicly regarding this myth: "We have no scriptural justification, however, for the belief that we had the privilege of choosing our parents and our life companions in the spirit world. This belief has been advocated by some, and it is possible that in some instances it is true, but it would require too great a stretch of the imagination to believe it to be so in all, or even in the majority of cases. Most likely we came where those in authority decided to send us. Our agency may not have been exercised to the extent of making choice of parents and posterity."[2]

In a letter written in 1971 to Elder Joe J. Christensen, who was then serving as associate commissioner for seminaries and institutes, the First Presidency reemphasized this point: "We have no revealed word to the effect that when we were in the preexistent state we chose our parents and our husbands and wives."[3]

Believing that we chose the person we would marry on earth while living in the premortal world can lead to a number of false conclusions. First, it might lead one to look for perfection, thinking that the "right one" would possess every quality we desire. Most people learn sooner or later that the "perfect person" is still a work-in-progress. Second, some people may spend their entire lives looking for the right person and pass by a number of others who could have made a wonderful companion. Third, there might be a temptation to ask the question "Is this the one?" about each person they meet. This places all kinds of pressures on dating relationships because, rather than forming friendships, the major motive is to discover if this is the person already chosen.

Myth 2: There is only one person with whom I could be happy.

On the contrary, there may be a number of people with whom you could be happy. President Spencer W. Kimball has said: "'Soulmates' are fiction and an illusion; and while every young man and young woman will seek with all diligence and prayerfulness to find a mate with whom life can be most compatible and beautiful, yet it is certain that almost any good man and good woman can have happiness and a successful marriage if both are willing to pay the price."[4]

One of my students told me that in the space of three months she had had three returned missionaries propose to her. Each said he had received an impression from the Lord that she was the one! Given the above statements, how could this happen? According to what Church leaders have taught, the three young men should have said to her, "I have received an impression that you are someone I *could* marry." What these young men neglected to consider was this young woman's freedom to choose. Perhaps they thought by sharing this information it would help persuade her to accept a marriage proposal. Remember, we cannot "make" another love us. God respects our agency and the agency of others. The marriage decision is such a serious one that both individuals should feel that the relationship is right for marriage.

Elder Dallin H. Oaks emphasized this when he said, "I have heard of cases where a young man told a young woman she should marry him because he had received a revelation that she was to be his eternal companion. If this is a true revelation, it will be confirmed directly to the woman if she seeks to know. In the meantime, she is under no obligation to heed it. . . . The man can receive revelation to guide his own actions, but he cannot properly receive revelation to direct hers. She is outside his stewardship."[5]

Myth 3: God will give you a dramatic revelation that you are to marry a certain person.

A young woman told me she was preparing to receive her patriarchal blessing. I asked her what she was doing to prepare herself for the experience. She said she was praying to be in tune with the blessing and was also praying for the patriarch that he would be inspired to tell her whom she should marry. In this mistaken hope, she was like a lot of people, who believe they must receive some grand or spectacular revelation before they marry. Though some may have a spiritual experience in this regard, such is not necessarily true for everyone. Believing that a divine signal is essential and not receiving it can cause some to become discouraged.

I know of a young man who said he had received a special revelation that he was to marry a particular girl. He shared this insight with her, but she declined his proposal. The young man then became discouraged, got mad at God for not giving her a similar revelation, and ultimately became inactive in the Church.

Elder James E. Faust said: "Occasionally someone suggests it be appropriate to have a computer dating program set up under church auspices, or some kind of marriage search committee set up so that the Church could more directly be involved in marriage partner selection. My response to such suggestions is that the selection process for eternal companions is so sacred that no one can or should intrude into the making of these choices except the individuals themselves, who should assume and bear that responsibility with divine guidance, parental counsel, and in some cases if necessary the help of a wise bishop."[6]

Elder Boyd K. Packer has counseled: "If you desire the inspiration of the Lord in this crucial decision, you must live the standards of the Church, and you must pray constantly for the wisdom to recognize those qualities upon which a successful union may be based. You must do the choosing, rather than to seek for some one-and-only so-called soul mate, chosen for you by someone else and waiting for you. You are to do the choosing. You must be wise beyond your years and be humbly prayerful unless you choose amiss."[7]

Elder Henry B. Eyring shared a personal experience that illustrates the effort we must exert to receive revelation. He couldn't seem to receive an answer to a problem he needed to solve. He went to President Harold B. Lee for advice. "He received me in a kindly way. In my anxiety, I soon blurted out my question: 'President Lee, how do I get revelation?' He smiled. I am glad he didn't laugh, since it was an odd question to ask. But he answered my question with a story. He said that during World War II he had been part of a group studying the question 'What should the Church be doing for its members in the military service?' He said they conducted interviews at bases up and down the country. They had data gathered. They had the data analyzed. They went back for more interviews. But still, no plan emerged.

"Then he gave me this lesson, which I now give to you, in about these words, 'Hal, when we had done all we knew how to do, when we had our backs to the wall, then God gave us the revelation. Hal, if you want to get revelation, do your homework.'"[8]

Perhaps there is no decision you will make in mortality that will have such long-term consequences yet at the same time requires the use of your agency to such a degree. The Lord expects you to approach this decision with the greatest reverence and care. Such a decision cannot be made quickly because it carries with it eternal consequences. While some couples may receive a powerful revelation that they are to marry, my experience has been that for many people it is a calm feeling that God approves of their choice.

Myth 4: As long as I marry in the Church, I won't have marriage problems.

I have known people who married to escape an abusive home or to solve financial concerns. Getting married is not like being given an Aladdin's magical lamp. What we are before marriage, we will generally be after marriage. Should we have major problems before, marriage will not erase them. In fact, being married may magnify them! Whether we marry in the Church or out, making a successful marriage requires shared commitment, hard work, patience, and love.

Myth 5: After we are married, I will be able to change the behavior of my marriage partner.

This is probably the most common erroneous assumption people have before and after marriage. Typically, newlyweds (and even sea- soned couples) work diligently to change the other while resolutely refusing to make any changes themselves. I have actually known people who behaved exactly the opposite of what their partner wanted just to demonstrate who was controlling the relationship! We have more control over ourselves than we do over anyone else, and the truth is, the only person you can truly change is you. The best way, then, to change your partner is to change yourself.

Let me share an example of what I mean. John and Alice had been dating steadily for five months. Though they weren't yet formally engaged, they were moving in that direction. However, there was one thing about Alice that was annoying to John and that was that she was habitually late for appointments. John had begun to nag her about it, and it was becoming a source of real contention between them.

Recognizing after a time that nagging was getting him nowhere, John decided to stop criticizing Alice and to instead be more kind and patient with her. It didn't take very long for Alice to notice John's considerate behavior and that he had discontinued harping about her tardiness. In a spirit of love and gratitude, Alice voluntarily decided to make a more concerted effort to be on time for appointments.

Myth 6: We will marry and then automatically live happily ever after.

Sometimes I hear young people say, "I want to marry someone who will make me happy." My response is: "No one is responsible for making you happy! Happiness in marriage is more about giving than receiving."

Dr. Shirley R. Klein, associate professor of family sciences at BYU, remembers a student who, on the last day of their course on marriage, brought a banner that read, "Marriage Is a Job!" Dr. Klein says, "You don't just get married and live happily ever after. Like your paid work, you need to work at marriage every single day."[9] In other words, we can live happily ever after—if we are willing to work at it—primarily by working to make our partner happy.

As you've read this chapter, you've probably noticed that most of the marriage myths have to do with placing responsibility on other people for our success and happiness in marriage. In reality, your happiness is determined by the choices you make. Our Father in Heaven will help us with this most important decision if we are willing to do our part in the selection process and if we are willing to change ourselves.

Assignment

Think about your own personality, habits, and preferences. Identify which of these traits is likely to present a problem in a marriage relationship. List the things you can modify in order to become a more compatible marriage partner. Work also to become more tolerant and patient in your relationships with family members, friends, and associates.

Section 1 Summary Points

1. The most important thing you will ever do is marry the right person, in the right place, by the right authority.

2. An eternal marriage is a Godlike marriage.

3. Keeping temple covenants is the key to achieving an eternal marriage.

4. To achieve an eternal marriage, you need to plan ahead by deciding what you will do and what you will not do.

5. Happy marriages are founded on personal righteousness and mutual commitment. Do not be deceived by the popular myths about love and marriage, which lead to false expectations and disappointment.

Becoming

THE RIGHT ONE

"Now is the time for you to plan good strong marriages and organize your

programs and set your standards and solidify your determination to prepare

for that married period of your lives which will be beautiful and rewarding"

(President Spencer W. Kimball, *Ensign*, Jan. 1975, 4).

CHAPTER 4

The Law of the Harvest

*"Whatsoever a man soweth, that shall he
also reap"(Galatians 6:7).*

Someone has said that we are not just "human beings," we are
"human becomings."

I am fascinated by the word *becoming*. It communicates growth,
change, and hope. It is a key word in preparation for marriage. There
is another word with reference to marriage preparation that, if we are
not careful, can take our focus away from *becoming* the right one. This
word is *looking*—looking for the right one. When this becomes our
focus, we might neglect "becoming" the right one. Let me illustrate.

One day while attending college I walked into the dorm room of a
fellow student. He had tacked on the wall a piece of paper that he
had entitled "My Dream Girl." He had listed on the paper the qualities he was looking for in the girl he wanted to marry. The list
included:

- College graduate
- Returned missionary
- Good-looking
- Good personality

I asked him where he thought he might find such a girl. His
response was most interesting: "Somewhere out there she is preparing
herself so that when we meet she will be ready." My first reaction was,
"How self-centered! What are *you* doing to prepare yourself for her?"

From this experience and many others like it, I have learned that it is more important to *be* the right one than to *find* the right one. President Ezra Taft Benson said it this way: "If you desire a fine companion, you should be that kind of fine person for whom that companion would be looking."[1]

We take into a relationship the sum total of who we are—our positive and negative character traits, our habits, attitudes, and the relationship skills we have acquired. The better prepared you are for marriage, the greater the chances that your marriage will be happy.

Someone has said, "Birds of a feather flock together." And it's true; there seems to be a law at work when it comes to the comfort we enjoy when we are with various people. I call this the "law of attraction." Simply stated it is: we tend to attract and be attracted to people who are similar to us. For example, if you want to marry someone with a strong testimony, then get a strong testimony yourself. If you want to marry someone who is generous and kind, practice being kind and generous yourself. If you want to marry someone who is worthy to enter the temple, then you be worthy.

Elder L. Aldin Porter of the First Quorum of the Seventy told of an experience he had with Elder Bruce R. McConkie. Elder McConkie had just been called as a General Authority and was touring the mission where Elder Porter was serving as a full-time missionary. He and his companion were driving Elder McConkie to a meeting. During the trip one of the elders asked Elder McConkie, "How can we know whom we should marry?"

Elder McConkie asked them to turn to D&C 88:40 and read it out loud. "For intelligence cleaveth unto intelligence; wisdom receiveth wisdom; truth embraceth truth; virtue loveth virtue; light cleaveth unto light; mercy hath compassion on mercy and claimeth her own . . ."

Elder Porter continued, "Elder McConkie explained to us that if we were men who loved the truth, we would be attracted to others who loved the truth. If we were men of virtue, we would attract others who were virtuous. If we loved light and justice and mercy, we would be attracted to a person who also loved these qualities. He then said, 'If you are men who love truth and virtue, go and find a young lady with these attributes and then proceed to fall in love.'"[2]

Perhaps this does not sound very romantic, but it is the key to marriage preparation. Your greatest concern, therefore, should be: "Am I becoming the type of person who will attract the type of person I would want to marry?" You don't need to concern yourself with looking for the perfect mate. What you do need to do is become the right one. The girl or boy of your dreams may cross your path and not recognize you if you are not qualified!

President David O. McKay has said that your preparation for marriage does not begin at the marriage altar but started "during the brilliant, fiery days of youth."[3] Each choice you have made and are making right now has contributed and is continuing to contribute to the type of marriage and family you will one day have. As you prepare, you need to understand and be aware of the "law of the harvest"— "Whatsoever a man soweth, that shall he also reap" (Galatians 6–7). Related to marriage, this law simply stated is, "You reap the results of your choices." President Spencer W. Kimball confirmed that this is an eternal law, saying that "the law of the harvest is ever in evidence."[4]

This law is in effect right now in your life. It can be said another way, "What you do now in your youth, you will reap in your marriage." King David sowed immorality and reaped sorrow all the rest of his life. Laman and Lemuel chose not to follow their prophet father and led a nation away from the Lord. Joseph, who was sold into Egypt, remained faithful to his covenants and eventually reaped a wonderful harvest.

President Howard W. Hunter has given us this solemn warning and a marvelous promise: "If you are dishonest in your dealings, if you cheat in your examinations, you are sowing the seeds of slavery and you will reap that harvest though you might rationalize to yourself, 'I am free.' If you are involved in necking and petting and immoral practices, you are becoming enslaved to your own passions and appetites, even though in your self-justifying pride you may say, 'I am free.' If you, yourself, resist these satanic temptations and determine to pay the daily price, to live the Law of the Harvest by clean, moral thoughts and practices, by upright, honest dealings, by integrity and conscientiousness in your studies, by fasting, prayer and worship, you will reap the harvest of freedom and inner peace and prosperity."[5]

What does the Law of the Harvest mean to you? Now is the time to carefully evaluate what you are doing to prepare yourself for marriage and an eternal family. The purpose of this section is to help you evaluate your preparation. You will examine five areas of your life: physical, social, mental, emotional, and spiritual. You will find that you have already sown many positive, wonderful habits in your life. You will probably also find some areas you may want to change. We will also look at how the atoning sacrifice of Jesus Christ can assist in our efforts to become the kind of person we desire.

Remember, until you are qualified, the person you may want to marry might cross your path and not be interested in you!

Assignment

1. Make a list of the qualities you would like in your eternal companion.

2. Identify those things on this list you need to acquire in order to attract such a person.

3. Choose one thing in your behavior to eliminate and one trait to cultivate in your effort to become a more eligible marriage partner and then go to work on these things.

CHAPTER 5

Prepare Yourself Physically and Socially

*"And Jesus increased in wisdom and stature, and in
favour with God and man" (Luke 2:52).*

Many of the problems people have in marriage can be traced to
habits they acquired in their youth. Psychologists tell us that
much of our personality is formed by age seven. Perhaps that is why
Alma counseled his son Helaman: "O, remember, my son, and learn
wisdom in thy youth; yea, learn in thy youth to keep the commandments of God" (Alma 37:35).

We take into marriage habits and attitudes that either build or tear
down relationships. For example, people who have developed negative physical appetites such as overeating, laziness, or lust will have
problems in relationships. People who are shy and uncommunicative
will generally find it more difficult to develop relationships. People
who have low feelings of self-worth will find it difficult to love and
serve others. Putting it candidly, to be successful as a marriage partner, we must learn to control our lives, our habits, attitudes, and
desires. Let's look at three areas that can help you better prepare for
marriage: learning to accept and control your physical body, learning
to work hard, and becoming socially well-rounded.

Learn to Accept and Control Your Physical Body

Your physical body is a sacred stewardship God has entrusted to
you, and you will be held accountable for how you treat it. He has

said in no uncertain terms that our body is a temple (see 1 Corinthians 3:16). In Doctrine and Covenants 93:35 the Lord speaks of the importance of our body. "The elements [of our physical body] are the tabernacle of God; yea, man is the tabernacle of God, even temples; and whatsoever temple is defiled, God shall destroy that temple."

Many young people are unhappy with their physical appearance. Part of the problem is that advertising agencies and media depictions have created an unrealistic standard of comparison. Very few individuals possess a face or physique that match those chosen to model clothing, advertise hair preparations or cosmetics, or attract attention to consumer goods in magazines, on posters, or on television. If our happiness depends on having the perfect body or face, almost everyone is destined to be unhappy.

The desire to be better looking or more attractive is especially strong in the teenage and young adult years, when so much emphasis is placed on physical appearance. The reality is, however, that for all but a few, our body structure will never be exactly what we want it to be! Rather than envy those few who have been genetically favored, we should strive to develop an attitude of gratitude for health and strength and the miracle of life. If we must envy someone, envy those who accept the hand that genetics has dealt them and who have learned to be comfortable in and be grateful for the body they have been given. Change what you can change and learn to accept what you can't change.

For example, I always wanted to be taller so that I could be better at sports. I soon learned that I needed to accept what I couldn't change and work on those elements of my body over which I had some control—weight, strength, and conditioning.

"How," you might ask, "will controlling my physical body prepare me for marriage?" Physical health and self-control have a direct relationship to how we feel, think, look, and act. If we are frequently sick or tired due to poor physical health, it will directly impact marital happiness. Someone who, because of poor eating habits or careless hygiene, is sick all the time is no fun to live with.

Learning to control your physical body and your appetites should be a major priority in your life. In this area some follow the path of least resistance. I know many young people who abuse their physical body: They go to bed late; they are addicted to junk foods and drinks; they have acquired the habit of laziness and have become addicted to television. I have heard some married women say, "My husband thinks he's sealed to the television set for time and eternity!" If you have any of these addictions, you must learn to overcome them or they will affect your marriage. So, how do you learn to control your physical body? Here are seven suggestions:

1. **Get some aerobic exercise at least three times a week for thirty minutes. To accomplish this, consider the following:**

   a. Choose a variety of exercises you enjoy such as walking, jogging, etc.
   b. Exercise to music you like. Research shows that working out to music increases the desire to exercise.
   c. Choose the best time of day for you and be consistent.
   d. Work out with a friend.

What are the benefits to you if you choose to exercise regularly?

- You will feel better mentally and emotionally.
- You will sleep better.
- Your cravings for fats and sugars will decrease.
- Your metabolic rate will increase, which will help you burn fat and lose weight should you need to.
- You will feel a sense of confidence because you are in control of your physical body.

2. **At least three times a week, engage in exercises that work your muscles.**

Doing sit-ups and push-ups and lifting weights is important to a well-rounded exercise program. For more information, see a qualified exercise consultant.

3. **Eat regular meals and have a balanced diet.**

Many young people develop the habit of skipping meals and then, when they eat, of eating a lot of nonnutritional foods such as pastries, sweets, and sodas. It's as one missionary said when asked what the four basic food groups were. He replied, "Peanut butter, Hostess chocolate cupcakes and Twinkies, chocolate milk, and Ramen noodles!"[1] You have already heard of the Law of the Harvest—what you sow now you will reap later. Look at it this way—what you *eat* now will *show* later! What we eat also has a direct impact on how we feel. If you can learn to eat foods that are good for you, the practice will benefit your life and your marriage. One of the messages of the Word of Wisdom is that God expects us to carefully choose what we take into our bodies.

4. Get adequate rest so you can arise early.

Many young people go to bed late and get up early. In doing so, they regularly burn the candle at both ends. Such a lifestyle affects a body's ability to resist disease as well as to think clearly. There are two extremes that should be avoided: getting too little rest and getting too much rest. Both of these can have a negative effect on how we feel. Too little rest can cause us to feel constantly tired and irritable. Too much rest can cause us to feel sluggish and slow. Each of us must get to know his or her own body and learn to practice self-discipline.

Elder Harold B. Lee gave the following advice to a newly called Assistant to the Quorum of the Twelve, Elder Marion G. Romney: "If you are to be successful as a General Authority, you will need to be inspired. You will need to receive revelation. I will give you *one* piece of advice: *Go to bed early and get up early.* If you do, your body and mind will become rested and then in the quiet of those early morning hours, you will receive more flashes of inspiration and insight than at any other time of the day."

Elder Romney said, "From that day on, I put that counsel into practice, and I know it works. Whenever I have a serious problem, or some assignment of a creative nature with which I hope to receive the influence of the Spirit, I always receive more assistance in the early morning hours than at any other time of the day. Following that counsel has helped me a great deal through the years."[2]

5. Learn to fast with a purpose.

It has been said that there is a big difference between going without food and fasting. Fasting with a purpose is a great way to develop self-discipline and to invite the Spirit of God to assist us in learning to control our appetites.

6. Learn to give thanks to God.

I learned a valuable lesson from an LDS Social Services counselor. While addressing a group of young men, he led a discussion on how to control our physical body and control impure thoughts and desires. He counseled them that in the moment of temptation, to remember all that they were thankful for. He said that when we recount our blessings there is a strength that comes to help us resist the desires of the flesh.

7. Practice good personal hygiene.

The Lord also expects us to take care of our body. Good grooming and good personal hygiene are very important if we wish to be attractive to members of the opposite sex. I have known some young people who seem to be totally oblivious to the need to bathe or shower regularly, wash their hair, brush their teeth, or use deodorant! Little wonder that they can't get a date, let alone a marriage proposal!

Learn to Work Hard

I've known some people who have entered marriage without ever having learned to do physical or mental labor. It requires work to succeed at marriage and handle all its demands. While growing up, some young people depend entirely on their parents to do everything; but in a marriage, someone has to hold a job, care for children, do the laundry, clean the house, do the shopping, take out the garbage, keep up the yard, pay the bills, maintain the vehicles, and do every other task that comes with maintaining a home and family. One of the greatest legacies my father left me was a work ethic. Too many young people today have not learned to work, or more important, not learned to *enjoy* work. You see them jumping from one job to another or always complaining that life is just too hard. When such a person gets married, it throws a tremendous burden on their partner and almost always leads to discord and unhappiness. So, as you prepare for marriage, do yourself a favor—learn to enjoy work.

Social Development

Social relationships are important here in mortality and in eternity. The Prophet Joseph Smith taught, "That same sociality which exists among us here will exist among us [in the hereafter], only it will be coupled with eternal glory, which glory we do not now enjoy" (D&C 130:2).

Marriage and family life are social experiences that are enhanced if we have learned to get along with people. From the moment of birth we learn that most of the happiness or sorrow we have in life is a product of relationships. As we grow and mature we develop social characteristics that either draw people to us or repel them. If we have good social skills, we can widen our circle of friends, thus giving us more opportunities to meet and date.

People who are extremely shy or antisocial usually find it more difficult to attract an eternal companion. At the other end of the spectrum are people who are overly aggressive, sometimes offensive, or who come on too strong. Elder Boyd K. Packer described what can happen to a relationship when there is insensitivity to the other person: "There is a phenomenon involved in courtship that is as strange as anything in human behavior. When a boy and a girl start to relate to one another, if the boy feels a heavy attraction for a girl and pursues her too strongly, surely he will be repulsed. And if a girl is too forward with a boy to whom she is attracted, he will reject her immediately. About all she has to do is telephone him twice and that ends that. While it is absolutely necessary that this deep attraction take place, if one or the other of the partners makes an expression of it too soon, the relationship is destroyed. In the early stages of courtship, if that happens, we say something like this: 'I can't stand anybody who really wants me.'"[3]

What do you do then when you really like someone? Be very careful to respect his or her feelings. Restrain yourself from pursuing the relationship too quickly. Be patient and allow the relationship to develop naturally into a good friendship. Avoid at all costs kissing too early or too much.

What do you do if you date very little or not at all? First, stick to your standards. That is the most important thing you can do. There is no benefit worth compromising your morals or cheapening your behavior. Anyone you attract through such a strategy will not respect you.

Second, try to increase your circle of friends. Make yourself accessible to other people. What are you doing to meet new people? Are you going to church, attending an institute of religion, or going to dances? You may need to move to a place where there are more Latter-day Saints your age. Many of my students, who have had few prospects, have changed their location or done something else to enlarge their circle of friends and in doing so have found their eternal companion. You may need to get out of your comfort zone by becoming more outgoing and friendly.

Third, analyze your personality to see if there are things that might need changing. Speaking at a women's conference, President Spencer W. Kimball asked those in attendance who wanted to be married but who had not yet found a spouse to consider the following: "You might take a personal inventory of your habits, your speech, your appearance, your weight, if it is heavier than most people appreciate, and your [annoying habits], if you have them. Take each item and analyze it. . . . Then go to work. Classify them, weigh them, corral them, and eliminate one at a time until you are a very normal person. . . . It is not likely that anyone will propose to you out of a sense of duty. You must do something about it."[4]

I have occasionally asked my institute students, active LDS young men and young women, to identify the characteristics or behaviors that serve as social turn-offs. Among their responses are the following:

What Girls Say They Dislike in a Boy

- Not active in church
- Dishonest
- Puts others down—judgmental

- Shallow—cares too much about how he looks and how girls look
- Expects a girl to wait on him, make him happy, the macho image
- Inconsistent behavior—nice one day, ignores you the next
- Too aggressive physically—does not respect the girl's values or feelings
- Takes the girl for granted, forgets the little things such as opening doors or being sensitive to her feelings
- Bad habits—smoking, drinking, etc.

What Boys Say They Dislike in a Girl

- Overly loud and/or crude
- Plays games—not honest with real feelings
- Immature—acts like a teenager
- Poor personal hygiene or overly made-up
- Overly emotional—overreacts to everything
- Too forward—assumes too much too soon, starts pressing the relationship too quickly
- Manipulative—gossips or backbites
- Not dependable—not on time, does not follow through
- An airhead—can't talk intelligently, no substance
- Flaunts her intelligence

Fourth, become anxiously engaged in life. Find some new interests, expand your awareness, be up and doing. At the same time, strive to increase your level of spirituality. Responding to the question "How can you develop a healthy dating relationship?" one sister wrote: "Through trial and error, I have found that developing a healthy dating relationship with someone requires that both people have a healthy relationship with God, which they maintain through prayer, scripture study (especially of the Atonement), repentance, and living the commandments."

If you cannot immediately find such a person, then be friends with everyone and follow this counsel from President Gordon B. Hinckley given during the April 1997 general conference: "Do not give up hope. And do not give up trying. But do give up being obsessed with it. The chances are that if you forget about it and become anxiously engaged in other activities, the prospects will brighten immeasurably."[5]

Fifth, learn to be sensitive to other people. One of my favorite professors when I attended BYU was sociologist Reed Bradford. Brother Bradford had a profound influence on my life and taught me many wonderful principles. One of his teachings was to be aware of what he called "the sensitive line." By this he meant that in relationships there is a line that, when crossed, offends or hurts the other person. This line is different for each person. Some are offended by sarcastic humor, others by excessive familiarity or intrusions into their privacy. The key to establishing friendly relationships is to be sensitive to the preferences of our associates and to be respectful of their feelings.

Remember, as you prepare yourself to be "the right one," it is important to "be in shape"—both socially and physically.

Assignment

1. Complete the following personal inventory charts, which are adapted from Brother Dee Hadley's book *Update*.[6]

2. Since we often don't see ourselves clearly, it might be helpful to have one or two people who know you well fill them out for you—perhaps a parent (the one who would be the most candid) and a close friend. With this information you can begin to look at areas where you might need to improve.

3. Fill out Personal Inventory Chart 1. In column 1 of the chart, put a check beside each of the ten characteristics that best describe who you are. In column 2 check the characteristics that are least descriptive of who you are.

4. When you have completed the first chart, fill out Personal Inventory Chart 2. In column 1, again check the ten traits that best describe you, and in column 2 check the ten least descriptive traits. Chart 1 will help you identify the positive aspects of your personality. Chart 2 will give you an idea of what you might need to change.

Personal Inventory Chart 1

1	2		1	2	
		Accepting			Gives praise readily
		Adaptable			Good listener
		Adventurous			Hard worker
		Affectionate			Helpful
		Beautiful			Honest
		Bighearted			Industrious
		Calm			Likes to make others happy
		Careful about appearance			Methodical
		Careful about money			Neat, orderly
		Charitable			Obedient
		Committed			Optimistic
		Communicative			Outgoing
		Compassionate			Positive
		Compliant			Respectful
		Concerned about feelings of others			Responsible
		Cooperative			Self-confident
		Courteous			Self-controlled
		Creative			Self-respecting
		Dependable			Sense of humor
		Detail oriented			Sensitive
		Dutiful			Sentimental
		Easy going			Sociable
		Efficient			Spiritual
		Encouraging			Sympathetic
		Enthusiastic			Tactful
		Even-tempered			Tender
		Expects to be treated kindly			Thoughtful
		Forgiving			Trusting
		Frank, forthright			Understanding
		Fun-loving			Varied interests
		Generous			Well-mannered
		Genuine			Willing worker

Personal Inventory Chart 2

1	2		1	2	
		Absent-minded			Jealous
		Afraid			Lazy
		Angry			Loud
		Anxious for approval			Moody
		Argumentative			Nagging
		Closed			Narrow-minded
		Competitive			Negative
		Complaining			Nervous
		Conceited			Overly aggressive
		Critical of others			Overly emotional
		Demanding			Overly neat
		Dependent			Overly sensitive
		Depressed			Overly talkative
		Dictatorial			Overly trusting
		Distant			Pessimistic
		Dogmatic			Phony
		Domineering			Possessive
		Easily discouraged			Procrastinates
		Easily excited			Radical
		Easily hurt			Rebellious
		Easily swayed			Resentful
		Extravagant			Rude
		Feels inferior			Sarcastic
		Gossipy			Sassy
		Hostile			Self-centered
		Hypersensitive			Self-indulgent
		Impatient			Shy
		Impractical			Stubborn
		Impulsive			Submissive
		Inconsiderate			Teasing
		Indiscreet			Touchy
		Insecure			Uncommunicative
		Insensitive			Uninvolved
		Intolerant			Untidy
		Irritable			Untruthful

CHAPTER 6

Becoming Mentally and Emotionally Mature

"With his stripes we are healed" (Mosiah 14:5).

A friend of mine shared with me the story of her son, a young man I'll call Tom. Tom married a young woman he had known for a few years. Two of those years he had been on a mission. During their dating and courtship, his fiancée was upbeat and happy and seemed to be a very positive person. But during the first week of their marriage, Tom started to see behavior in her he had never seen before. She would be unexplainably angry one day and pleasant the next. Now, after many years of marriage, he continues to struggle to accommodate her unpredictable behavior and is very unhappy. Because of her anger and moodiness, she has alienated not only Tom but also their children. Tom's wife refuses to take responsibility for her emotional illness, blaming it instead on her family.

The mother ended her sad story by saying that young people need to really get to know the person they want to marry. The girl's family had warned her son before he got married by saying, "She's not always happy and positive like you think." But he didn't listen. Get to know the person's family, and listen to what others say. Dr. Brent Barlow has said, "Start out with stability in your own life. Take two stable people, and then start a relationship."[1] Immaturity is an obstacle to building a successful marriage. The more mature you are mentally and emotionally, the happier you are likely to be in a marriage relationship.

A *Peanuts* cartoon pictured Snoopy the dog talking to himself: "Sometimes when I get up in the morning, I feel very peculiar. I feel like I've just got to bite a cat! I feel like if I don't bite a cat before sundown, I'll go crazy! But then I just take a deep breath and forget about it. That's what is known as real maturity!"

Each of us takes into a relationship the positive and negative characteristics we have accumulated over the years. Some people have many more problems than others. Marriage will not cause these problems to disappear, nor does it automatically confer maturity on people. In fact, because being married can be very stressful, it can intensify our emotional challenges.

Take for example the situation of John. John had always had a very bad temper. His fiancée had seen some evidence of that during their courtship, but she thought that with the responsibility of marriage, John would change. She was devastated to learn, after marriage, that John's temper was even worse than she had suspected. John would have been wise to have sought help in solving his anger problem before getting married.

Immaturity

One of the reasons for problems in marriage is that kids often marry kids. By this I mean that two immature people meet and marry. Elder Mark E. Petersen, until his death in 1984 a member of the Quorum of the Twelve, said: "Immaturity in marriage leads to disaster. Do not marry unless you intend to make it permanent. Both parties must decide and agree to make it work regardless of the obstacles that may arise. To do that they must eliminate selfishness. These are among the main reasons for divorce—particularly among younger couples. In other words, a person contemplating marriage must be willing to grow up before they get married."[2]

None of us behaves in a perfectly mature manner all the time, no matter what our age. However, some people are much better prepared for marriage than others. Some, as Elder Petersen said, need to grow up! Our degree of maturity or immaturity is revealed when we are in stressful situations. Mature people understand their feelings and deal with them in positive ways. William C. Menniger, a noted marriage and family therapist, wrote: "No one can go through life without being under tension at one time or another. All of us experience anxious moments about a situation or a problem. We all get panicky over uneasy feelings and often are unable to face our problems objectively. But the more mature we are, the better we will understand these feelings. We will know that at times we will become confused and may behave in unreasonable ways. Our maturity depends, to a certain extent, on how well we can handle our problems and how easily we can turn the tenseness that often accompanies problems into productive outlets."[3]

My experience is that immature people are focused mainly on themselves and on the present. They do not think of what they can give to a relationship but what they can get from it. "What have you done for me lately?" is their constant concern. Mature people, on the other hand, see a relationship as an opportunity to give something to another. They have learned to be sensitive to the feelings of others and to control their own. They make decisions based on what will be best for the future and not what is expedient at the moment. One way to look at it is to compare a mature adult with a child. Children are usually very emotionally immature, and some so-called "adults" can also be very "childish."

Childish Attitudes/Behavior	*Mature Attitudes/Behavior*
1. Usually wants his or her own way.	Has learned to compromise and negotiate with others.
2. Lives for the present; wants things right now.	Can postpone immediate wants for future goals.
3. Is temperamental and easily upset; pouts.	Can control emotions; is even-tempered in expressing feelings.
4. Is overly dependent on others.	Can be happy no matter what others do.

5. Acts impulsively.	Thinks things through before acting.
6. Is irresponsible, undependable.	Accepts responsibility and follows through—can be counted on.
7. Resists authority and counsel.	Seeks advice and counsel from others.

As you review this chart, you will probably notice an area or two where you might need to become more mature. This is normal, but the more mature you are, the greater the chance you will be a good marriage partner.

Often, immaturity is a result of not being able to deal with our emotions. The teenage and young adult years are characterized by extreme emotional highs and lows. These swings are often caused by conflicts between boy- or girlfriends, roommates, or parents or other authority figures. It is not uncommon for young people to say, "Life sucks!" and the next day feel great about life. All it takes to change an outlook is a perceived slight, a harsh word, or even a dirty look.

When young people complain about problems in a relationship, I try to help them see that they can learn a lot from such experiences. As we mature, we begin to control to a greater degree the intensity of our highs and lows. One young woman told me that she once stayed in her bedroom for two days straight, alternately sleeping and crying because a young man she liked had ignored her. Her life was completely destroyed because of another person!

In an effort to help, I asked her this question: "Are you going to allow the actions of one boy to determine your happiness?" I then said, "You are now learning what it means to grow up and to be able to confront the disappointments of life without letting them destroy you." I reminded her that she is a daughter of God and that He loves her very much—that she had been blessed with many gifts and talents and had a wonderful future. To her credit she accepted the advice I gave her: "Instead of moping in your bedroom, get out and do something. Try to make someone else happy, and as you do this you will stop feeling so sorry for yourself."

Immaturity is not a terminal disease; it is something people can grow out of as they gain experience in life. Note how a missionary or a college student who leaves home matures—often quickly becoming self-sufficient, responsible, and able to successfully manage his or her own affairs. Mental and emotional illnesses, however, present more serious challenges, and such conditions are not cured by simply growing up.

Though I am not a trained psychologist, I have met a number of young people who I believe were not mentally healthy. Here are some of the characteristics I have observed in these troubled people. This is certainly not an exhaustive list of symptoms, but these are some of the kinds of problems that if uncorrected can lead to serious challenges in a marriage.

People who are unhealthy mentally are excessively moody, depressed, and full of despair; they are often dishonest with themselves and with others; they cannot control their anger or feelings of jealousy; they are physically or emotionally abusive to others; they have extremely low feelings of self-worth; they are often addicted to drugs, alcohol, sex, gambling, shopping, or some other compulsive behavior; they are overly concerned about their personal appearance; and they often live in a dream world, unable to deal with reality.

Of the above symptoms, one of the most destructive to a happy, satisfying life is depression. This is not to say that you can't have a bad day occasionally. Everyone does, and Elder Boyd K. Packer has said: "It was meant to be that life would be a challenge. To suffer some anxiety, some depression, some disappointment, even some failure is normal. Teach our members that if they have a good, miserable day once in a while, or several in a row, to stand steady and face them. Things will straighten out. There is great purpose in our struggle in life."[4]

Someone who is not emotionally well may have extended periods of depression, lasting for indefinite periods of time. Those who suffer from chronic depression usually focus on themselves, to the exclusion of others.

On the other hand, those who are emotionally healthy are generally happy and optimistic about life; they are authentic, that is, honest with themselves and others; they are able to control their temper and feelings of jealousy; they face personal shortcomings and sins with hope and courage; they accept their physical body, changing what they can and living more or less contentedly with what they can't change. Because they are basically accepting of themselves, emotionally healthy people are interested in others and do not focus all their attention on their own problems or challenges.

Ask yourself a question. Of the two types of people described above, which is easier to have for a friend? Which one would you prefer to have for a marriage partner?

Physical Causes of Mental Illness

We are not exactly sure why some people have a predisposition to mental or emotional illness. In some cases it is the result of chemical imbalances within the body or brain. Anyone who experiences severe, prolonged depression should seek competent medical advice. A doctor can usually discover if such a condition is related to a physical problem or if an individual could benefit from counseling.

Our Family

In the Book of Mormon, much is made of the violent, hateful, and wicked behavior of the Lamanites, which is attributed in part to the incorrect "traditions of their fathers" (Mosiah 1:5), which is to say that behavioral patterns are passed from generation to generation, through heredity and/or example. The family into which we are born and the environment in which we are raised do have an effect. Tragically, negative behavioral patterns can be and are passed from one generation to the next, until someone recognizes what is happening and says, "This is where it stops! I will not pass this problem on to my children!" and takes steps to modify his or her behavior.

A baby enters the world totally dependent on others. Babies whose basic needs for love and acceptance are met usually develop positive, confident feelings about themselves and about life.[5] If, on the other hand, the baby does not receive the needed warmth and love, he or she may develop mental and emotional problems.[6] There is also evidence that the way parents discipline their children can influence the tendency to depression. Traumatic events experienced in one's youth can also have a profound impact on mental and emotional health. These traumas include but are not limited to physical, emotional, or sexual abuse; the death of a parent or other family member; the divorce of parents. Someone who has experienced physical or sexual abuse can be helped by first seeing their bishop and then, if necessary, receiving help from a competent counselor.

Our Own Disobedience

Many of the problems we experience are the result of our own choosing. For example, someone who is sexually promiscuous will one day have to deal with the guilt, the low feeling of self-worth, and the loss of the Spirit of God. One who is dependent on alcohol or drugs will have to deal with the problems of addiction and their negative effects on self-worth, interpersonal relationships, and health. We simply can't blame all of our problems on our genetic inheritance or on our environment. An old Chinese proverb says, "If you pick up one end of a stick, you also pick up the other end. If you choose the beginning of a road, you pick the end of the road."

Moral agency provides us with the freedom to choose but also requires us to endure the consequences of our choices. Sadly, when we are young we tend to exercise our agency without always looking down the road to where our choices will lead us. President Spencer W. Kimball has identified immoral behavior as one of the causes of mental and emotional illness: "Immorality brings generally a deep sense of guilt. These unresolved guilt complexes are the stuff from which mental breakdowns come, the building blocks of suicide, the fabric of distorted personalities, the wounds that scar or decapitate individuals or families."[7]

Living the gospel results in peace of mind and happiness. Continuing to willfully sin does not bring such peace. This is not to say that all mental or emotional challenges are a result of not living the gospel. As stated earlier, often they are a result of forces beyond our control. But whatever the cause, the gospel of Jesus Christ can assist us in the healing process. While addressing the topic of abuse, Elder Richard G. Scott offered this comforting counsel: "No matter what the source of difficulty and no matter how you begin to obtain relief—through a qualified professional therapist, doctor, priesthood leader, friend, concerned parent or loved one—no matter how you begin, those solutions will never provide a complete answer. The final healing comes through faith in Jesus Christ and His teachings, with a broken heart and a contrite spirit and obedience to His commandments. Do what you can do a step at a time. Seek to understand the principles of healing from the scriptures and through prayer. Above all, *exercise faith in Jesus Christ*. I testify that the surest, most effective, and shortest path to healing comes through application of the teachings of Jesus Christ in your life."[8]

As a young man, Alma the Younger experienced severe personal inner turmoil resulting from his own disobedience. He described his torment as "the pains of a damned soul." Note how, through Jesus Christ, he was healed: "And it came to pass that as I was thus racked with torment, while I was harrowed up by the memory of my many sins, behold, I remembered also to have heard my father prophesy unto the people concerning the coming of one Jesus Christ, a Son of God, to atone for the sins of the world.

"Now, as my mind caught hold upon this thought, I cried within my heart: O Jesus, thou Son of God, have mercy on me, who am in the gall of bitterness, and am encircled about by the everlasting chains of death.

"And now, behold, when I thought this, I could remember my pains no more; yea, I was harrowed up by the memory of my sins no more.

"And oh, what joy, and what marvelous light I did behold; yea, my soul was filled with joy as exceeding as was my pain!" (Alma 36:17–20).

Let me share the story of a young woman I will call Sally, who experienced the healing spoken of by Elder Scott.

Sally came from a very difficult background. Her parents divorced when she was a little girl, and afterward her father wanted very little to do with her. Her mother attempted to provide love and support but was often away from home due to her employment. The result was that Sally grew to young womanhood filled with some serious insecurities, and at a young age she became involved in the use of drugs and in immorality. Given what she was willing to do, she had little trouble finding boyfriends, but these relationships with young men were unsatisfactory and usually lasted only a short while.

After finishing high school, Sally went away to college, where she came in contact with some Latter-day Saint students who befriended her. She took the missionary discussions and was eventually baptized. Sally also enrolled in an institute class on preparing for celestial marriage, and while taking the class she came to realize that if she were to have a happy, successful life, she would need to deal with the insecurities she had always felt. She sought out her bishop, who explained how the help she needed had been provided by the Savior in the Atonement. Over time, with the bishop's guidance and the help of the Lord, Sally was able to make some significant changes in her outlook on life.

Consider the process Sally went through in dealing with the problems she faced:

First, she became aware that there were areas in her life where she was not healthy. In this she was extremely honest with herself. Though she came to understand that her family background had contributed to her insecurities, she was able to hope that she didn't need to remain forever trapped in her mindset—that with the Savior's help she could modify her outlook and behavior.

Second, she sought help from her bishop, who was able to guide her through her struggle to take charge of her life. With God's help, she was able to deal with her past problems and through the Atonement find a stability that had evaded her to that point.

I have known a number of young people who, like Sally, have come from challenging backgrounds but have been able to enjoy happy, successful marriages.

My own wife took quite a chance when she married me. Alcoholism ran in my family, and my parents divorced when I was young. I had acquired a number of insecurities in my youth. It was only through the gospel of Jesus Christ that I came to appreciate that I was a child of God and that, with the help of the Lord, my insecurities could be healed. My wife has also played a significant role in that process. Her love for me, coupled with my love for the Lord and for her, made it possible for me to make some significant and satisfying changes in my life.

Here is the point. Even though we enter marriage with some problems, whether it be immaturity (and we are all immature to a degree) or mental or emotional challenges (and we all have them to a greater or lesser degree), with the help of God and the help of a loving companion, we can have a happy marriage. There is hope for each of us! The key is to marry someone who loves us for who we are and who is understanding, kind, and patient. It goes without saying that you need to bring the same attributes to your marriage.

Assignment

Consider the following:

1. What can you do to become more mentally mature and emotionally healthy? In what ways can the Lord Jesus Christ assist you in this process? What can you do to draw closer to Him?

2. Read carefully 3 Nephi 9:13. What promise does the Lord give?

3. Read Ether 12:27. Is it possible to overcome our weaknesses? What or who is the source of our strength?

CHAPTER 7

Learning to Be Unselfish

"Repent of [your] pride and of [your] selfishness"
(D&C 56:8).

On their wedding day, the bride and groom usually have a high opinion of each other and feel they are totally in love. It has never occurred to them that they might not always feel the same way. Being in love seems so effortless; they give no thought to what it will take to make the marriage work or even that any work will be required. But it is possible that a few months or years later these same two people may be living in a condition of confusion and despair, unhappy in their relationship, and each blaming the other for the problems they are experiencing.

Is such a thing possible? Sad to say, yes. Some disillusioned newlyweds have said:

- "I found things about him or her after we were married that I hadn't seen before."
- "We went into marriage with false expectations."
- "We grew further and further apart until the love died."
- "We were so involved physically, we didn't see reality."

Prophets of God have identified selfishness as the main cause of marriage failure. President Spencer W. Kimball said: "Every divorce is the result of selfishness on the part of one or the other or both parties to a marriage contract. Someone is thinking of self-comforts, conveniences, freedoms, luxuries, or ease."[1]

President Gordon B. and Sister Marjorie Hinckley were interviewed on their sixtieth wedding anniversary. Sister Hinckley said, "You cannot be selfish in marriage. You have to have as your first priority the happiness and comfort of your spouse. If you work on that, then you are happy too." President Hinckley added, "Selfishness brings about conflict and all of the difficulties that afflict so many, many marriages. Being plain, downright selfish is the problem."[2]

Selfishness is defined as being concerned with one's own pleasure or well-being without regard for others. Selfish people are turned-in to themselves rather than turned-out to others. Elder Neal A. Maxwell characterizes selfish people as "takers," not "givers,"[3] and President David O. McKay taught that marriage "cannot survive selfishness."[4]

Your success in marriage, your future happiness, will be based to a great degree on how unselfish you are—whether you are a giver or a taker. Elder Theodore M. Burton, an emeritus General Authority, taught that most of the unhappiness in the world is the product of selfishness:

"True love is based on personal unselfishness, but our modern world does not seem to understand this. Modern man has lost his capacity to love. Jesus warned us that one of the principal characteristics of the last days would be that love among the people would gradually die. Jesus said, 'Because iniquity shall abound, the love of many shall wax cold' (Joseph Smith—Matthew 1:10). My thesis is that the iniquity of which he spoke is based on personal selfishness. That is the reason why love among the people is dying. . . . It may well be that the present attitude of personal selfishness is the cause of most of the unhappiness with life among the people of the world."[5]

Today, selfishness characterizes our society and is even more pronounced than when Elder Burton made the above statement. We live in a "me" centered society, glorified by many TV sitcoms and movies. Advertisers play on this theme with ads such as "You Deserve a Break Today" and "You're Number 1!" and "Indulge Yourself." Romance novels and magazines glorify material pleasure and personal gratification. While the media has influenced our self-centeredness, there are other factors.

President Ezra Taft Benson identified pride as "the universal sin" of our day. And "selfishness," he said, "is one of the more common faces of pride. 'How everything affects me' is the center of all that matters—self-conceit, self-pity, worldly self-fulfillment, self-gratification, and self-seeking."[6]

Some parents feel guilty because they both work and thus must leave their children in daycare centers. Trying to compensate for these feelings, they sometimes overindulge their children, and children who are raised in permissive homes are conditioned to be selfish. Elder Hugh B. Brown, former First Counselor in the First Presidency, said, "The child that is pampered in the home will expect to be pampered after marriage. Among the seeds of divorce one of the most prolific is over-indulgence. It grows into extreme selfishness."[7]

President Gordon B. Hinckley emphasized this when he said: "I am satisfied that a happy marriage is not a matter of romance as it is an anxious concern for the comfort and well-being of one's companion.

"Selfishness so often is the basis of money problems, which are a very serious and real factor affecting the stability of family life. Selfishness is at the root of adultery, the breaking of solemn and sacred covenants to satisfy selfish lust. Selfishness is the antithesis of love. It is a cankering expression of greed. It destroys self-discipline. It obliterates loyalty. It tears up sacred covenants. It afflicts both men and women.

"Too many who come to marriage have been coddled and spoiled and somehow led to feel that everything must be precisely right at all times, that life is a series of entertainments, that appetites are to be satisfied without regard to principle."[8]

Pride, pampered children, the media—all have contributed to the challenges we face today. And what are the results? Elder Theodore M. Burton said, "People become conditioned by this exposure and grow up expecting only personal gratification in marriage. Personal selfishness is the main reason for the present high divorce rate throughout the world."[9]

There is yet another factor you should consider. Most young people are by nature selfish. Most are not givers and are more concerned about self than anything else. For example, how often do teenagers voluntarily offer to help with the dishes or do housework? How often do they consider how their actions affect the feelings of others? How often do they thank their parents for what they do? This is one of the reasons why most teenage marriages end in divorce. To have a happy, successful marriage, you must make the transition from an immature attitude of *taking* to an unselfish attitude of *giving*. Sadly enough, many do not make this transition easily and face tremendous challenges in marriage until they learn to be givers.

How then can you become more unselfish? Elder Burton suggests that dating provides an opportunity to practice principles of generosity and courtesy. "What is the main purpose for dating? Isn't it to get to know another person well enough to know what kind of a partner that person would be? Isn't it to learn to know that other person's character, interests, talents, and abilities? Or is dating merely an opportunity to satisfy one's passions? Each person will have to answer that question for himself. However, a sure guide would be to follow the words of the Savior: 'Again I say unto you, let every man esteem his brother as himself' (D&C 38:25)."[10]

Consider for a moment how differently the giver and the taker approach dating.

Taker	*Giver*
"I hope he or she helps me to have a good time."	"What can I do to ensure my date has a good time?"
"I hope others see me with him or her."	"How can I get to know him or her better?"
"Will I get a little action?"	"Will this activity assist him or her to live the gospel?"
"How can I impress him or her?"	"Will this person be happy he or she went out with me?"

Elder Neal A. Maxwell has given this advice: "You and I will not go to sleep tonight without having confronted specific, if only minor, situations in which we can choose either to be selfish or selfless. Who will get his car out of the crowded parking lot first? Who will wait for whom at the busy doorway out of an auditorium? Which partner in a marriage (where there may have been a few harsh words today) will be selfless enough to take the verbal initiative necessary for reconciliation? Who will put out the light? Who will get up with a crying baby? Which student will still find time to thank a particular teacher or professor who deserves to be thanked for the quality of his teaching? Indeed, the very thought process that may be going on in your mind as you read probably finds you either envisioning such specific possibilities as may lie before you this very moment or becoming rather bored by the idea of immediacy and pending changes to be selfless."[11]

What are the blessings that can come to you as you learn to be an unselfish giver? Consider the following:

- Unselfishness is closely tied to humility and leads people to rely on the Lord.
- Unselfishness creates an attitude that looks for and notices the needs of others.
- Unselfishness helps people feel secure about themselves, freeing them from the need of receiving constant recognition.
- Unselfishness helps us appreciate God, life, others, and nature.
- Unselfishness helps us communicate better with others, for we want to listen and understand.
- Unselfishness causes us to consider carefully how our words and actions will affect others.
- Unselfishness, then, is the key to a happy, productive marriage.

Assignment

Consider the following questions, which will help you determine whether you are a giver or a taker.

1. Do I have a Church calling, and am I fulfilling it to the best of my ability?

2. Have I expressed appreciation to two people within the past week for things they have done for me?

3. Have I introduced myself within the past week to someone I have not known?

4. Have I done anything not expected of me for my parents, brothers,

sisters, or friends within the past month?

5. While praying, do I spend more time asking for things or thanking Heavenly Father for my blessings?

6. If I have a job, do I go the extra mile and do more than my employer requires?

7. Am I a loving person, or do I expect others to do everything for me?

8. Am I patient or impatient in my dealings with people I meet?

CHAPTER 8

Make the Lord Your First Priority

"Seek ye first the kingdom of God"
(Matthew 6:33).

Most active Latter-day Saints want to marry someone who is spiritual. Why? Because spirituality is the foundation of the gospel of Jesus Christ, and when this is in place, the chances of achieving an eternal marriage are much greater. But what is spirituality, and how do we acquire this important attribute? President David O. McKay defined spirituality as the "consciousness of victory over self, and of communion with the Infinite." He further explained, "[Spirituality] impels one to conquer difficulties and acquire more and more strength."[1] Then spirituality is an attribute that motivates us to want to do whatever the Lord asks of us.

A student once said to me that she wanted to marry a returned missionary who had 100 percent attendance at Church meetings. I suggested to her that a better gauge might be to marry a returned missionary who had 100 percent faith in the Lord. Outward compliance with Church teachings, such as attendance at meetings, is not necessarily an accurate indicator of spirituality. Activity means little if the activity is not prompted by righteous desires. Someone has pointed out that it is possible to "be active in the Church" but "not be active in the gospel." Sadly enough, some people have learned to say the right things, but their hearts are not right. True spirituality is an internal attribute and, a matter of the heart, and possessing it prompts us to do the right things for the right reasons.

I indicated earlier that Susan and I were married by Elder LeGrand Richards of the Quorum of the Twelve. As a result of that experience, we felt some attachment to him, and for Susan and me, Elder Richards and his wife were a great example of a spiritually minded married couple.

Brother Truman Madsen shared the story of how Elder LeGrand Richards proposed to his wife: Shortly after returning from his first mission, "He was walking along with her, and everything was well between them, when he said, 'Ina, there is someone who will always come before you.' She gasped. She cried out, and she ran. When LeGrand caught up with her, he stopped her and said: 'Wait, wait, you don't understand. On my mission there were times when the Lord was so close that I felt I could almost reach out and touch Him. He has to be the foundation of our lives; but, Ina, if you want to be second, I want to marry you.'"[2]

To be truly spiritual is to put the Lord first in our lives! President Ezra Taft Benson has assured us of the following: "When we put God first, *all other things fall into their proper place or drop out of our lives*. Our love of the Lord will govern the claims of our affection, the demands of our time, the interests we pursue, and the order of our priorities."[3]

President Marion G. Romney said that we can make every decision in our lives correctly if we can learn to be guided by the Spirit.[4] Anyone who wishes to be guided by the Spirit will do well to pray regularly and partake weekly of the sacrament.

An experience I had with a young man reminds me of the importance of constantly nourishing the Spirit in our lives. I received a telephone call one evening from a returned missionary who asked if I would visit with him. I had known him before his mission, when he was a participant in a stake young single adult Sunday School class I was teaching. When I met with him he said that he had been experiencing problems since returning home from his mission. "The major problem," he said, "is that I do not feel as close to the Lord as I did on my mission." I told him that in my experience, that was typical of many returned missionaries.

"But," I said, "you don't have to be a full-time missionary to be close to the Lord. What did you do on your mission to nurture your relationship with the Lord?" He said he had studied the scriptures every day.

"Are you doing that now?" I asked.

"No," he said, "I don't seem to have time to study."

What else did you do?

He replied that he had prayed and fasted regularly.

"Are you praying every day now?" I asked.

"No, I don't pray very often," he confessed.

"What did you do on Sundays?"

He responded, "I attended my meetings and tried to serve the Lord."

"Are you keeping the Sabbath day holy now?" I asked.

"Not completely."

"What about fasting?" I asked. "What did you fast for last fast Sunday?"

"Not really anything," he said.

"Was there anything else you did on your mission that made you feel close to the Spirit?"

"I served people."

"Do you have a calling now?"

"I'm a home teacher."

"How many families?"

"Three."

"Did you visit them last month?"

"No."

"When was the last time you bore your testimony?"

"In the mission field."

He was getting the point. If we wish to enjoy the influence of the Holy Spirit in our lives, we need to provide a compatible environment. That means saying our prayers, reading the scriptures, bearing testimony, keeping the Sabbath day holy, serving others, and living a righteous life.

President Howard W. Hunter said: "Developing spirituality and attuning ourselves to the highest influences of godliness is not an easy matter. It takes time and frequently involves a struggle. It will not happen by chance, but is accomplished only through deliberate effort and by calling upon God and keeping his commandments."[5]

Assignment

What are you doing to place the Lord first in your life?

1. Are you studying the scriptures regularly?

2. Are you praying daily?

3. Are you magnifying your Church calling?

4. Are you regularly attending sacrament and other meetings?

5. Are you paying a full tithing?

6. When was the last time you bore your testimony to a friend or in a meeting?

7. Are you striving to keep the commandments? Where do you need to improve your behavior?

8. Are you keeping the Sabbath day holy?

CHAPTER 9

Change What You Can Change

*"How great is his joy in the soul that
repenteth!" (D&C 18:13).*

I have heard many young people say, "I wish I were taller. I wish I were shorter. I wish I were prettier. I wish I were more like . . ."

The sad truth is, there are some things about us we simply can't change! These we must learn to accept. But the good news is that there are things we *can* change. That is the wonderful message of the gospel of Jesus Christ: "We can change!"

In a gospel context, that process is called repentance, and it is the process through which, with divine help, we can literally transform ourselves.

Most problems in relationships can be traced to changes that need to be made on the inside, not on the outside. The scriptures refer to this as undergoing "a change of heart." President Ezra Taft Benson contrasted two different approaches to change: "The Lord works from the inside out. The world works from the outside in. The world would take people out of the slums. Christ takes the slums out of people, and then they take themselves out of the slums. The world would mold men by changing their environment. Christ changes men, who then change their environment. The world would shape human behavior, but Christ can change human nature."[1]

People get angry because they can't control themselves. They have a difficult time saying "I'm sorry" because of pride. They are unfaithful because of lust. Each of these problems is a problem of the heart, which is a symbol for our innermost feelings and motivations. The Lord used this imagery when explaining to Joseph Smith why so few are chosen to serve: "Their *hearts* are set so much on the things of the world" (D&C 121:35; emphasis added).

How do we change our hearts and become converted? The word *convert* means to change. This conversion, or change, comes through and because of the atoning sacrifice of Jesus Christ, who has told us that if we will come unto him, he will heal us. Elder Richard G. Scott of the Quorum of the Twelve offered this encouragement to those seeking to change through repentance: "Please understand that the way back is not as hard as it seems to you now. Satan wants you to think that it is impossible. That is not true. The Savior gave His life so that you can completely overcome the challenges you face. (See 2 Nephi 2:6–8.)

". . . Lucifer will do all in his power to keep you captive. You are familiar with his strategy. He whispers: . . . 'You can't change; you have tried before and failed.' 'It's too late; you've gone too far.' Don't let him discourage you. . . .

"Your exercise of faith permits you to call upon the strength of the Lord when you need it. Obedience to His commandments allows that help to be given. The power of God will come into your life because of your faithful obedience to His commandments. . . .

"Don't confront your problem armed with only your own experience, understanding, and strength. Count on the infinite power of the Lord by deciding now to be obedient to His teachings. (See 2 Nephi 31:19–21.)

". . . I promise you, in the name of the Lord, that He will help you. He will be there in every time of need. He gave His life so that you can change your life. I promise you that you'll feel His love, strength, and support. Trust Him completely. He is not going to make any mistakes. He knows what He is doing. . . . Be obedient to His teachings, and He will bless you. I promise you He will bless you."[2]

Each individual takes into a relationship various habits and attitudes that will make it difficult to get along and that will need to be eliminated or changed. If during dating and courtship these irritating or difficult behaviors have been observed, most people enter marriage expecting their marriage partner will change. But one of the greatest lessons I have learned is that we have a much better chance of changing ourselves than of getting our loved one to change.

Here are some lessons I have learned about change:

First, making even a small change in our habits, behavior, or attitude is not easy! If we are to succeed, we must first genuinely desire to change and then earnestly call upon God for help. As we evaluate our needs, it might be helpful to recognize that in this area we really have only two choices:

- Blame others and remain the way we are.
- Acknowledge our problems and repent.

Should we choose to blame others, nothing will change. Such an attitude undermines true growth and is fatal to relationships.

Second, it often takes time to change. President Heber J. Grant was fond of quoting Ralph Waldo Emerson, who said, "That which we persist in doing becomes easier to do, not that the nature of the thing has changed but that our power to do has increased."[3] Relying fully on the Lord and being persistent is the key. President Ezra Taft Benson said, "Becoming Christlike is a lifetime pursuit and very often involves growth and change that is slow, almost imperceptible."[4]

Third, as we strive to change, Satan will try to discourage us. Discouragement is one of his greatest tools. The story is told about the devil holding a garage sale in which he offered for sale all of his tools except one. When asked why he held back that particular tool, the devil replied, "It is the tool of discouragement, and it is too useful to me. I can dispose of all my other tools, and with it alone I can accomplish my work."

Fourth, realize that through the Atonement of Jesus Christ we can not only be forgiven of sin, but we can also receive help to change. *Grace* has been defined as "divine help." The Lord can help us with our challenges. President Spencer W. Kimball has given us all this hope: "In abandoning evil, transforming lives, changing personalities, molding characters or remolding them, we need the help of the Lord, and we may be assured of it if we do our part. The man who leans heavily upon his Lord becomes the master of self and can accomplish anything he sets out to do, whether it be to secure the brass plates, build a ship, overcome a habit, or conquer a deep-seated transgression."[5]

Fifth, desiring to change or repent of those things that hold us back from truly loving God and others is essential to lasting relationships. That is why it is so important for us to love the Lord and to marry someone who loves the Lord. When He is at the center of a marriage relationship, couples can overcome most challenges they face.

Over the years, I have asked my students to write a paragraph on what the Atonement of Jesus Christ means to them. Here are some of their statements, which illustrate how we can change with the help of the Lord.

- "I make mistakes, and being imperfect, I am unable to return to God. However, the Atonement makes up for my imperfections and allows me to return to God. This gives my life purpose! This defines my existence. This means that there is a reason for my life, and a way by which it can continue—and not only continue, but receive joy, and eventually perfection."
- "No matter what the sin, and the grief that comes from that sin, there is forgiveness and peace on conditions of repentance. The Atonement to me brings true happiness knowing that I am square with the Lord or can be if I turn to Him. Peace has come into my life because of repentance."
- "It means that I get a second chance to do better, to be the best I can be, to learn from my mistakes."
- "Repentance. Wow . . . repentance. Oh, how He loves me, oh, how strong the bond between us. Oh, how sweet is His mercy. Oh, how I am indebted to Him. I *can* never forget, I could *never* forget, I *pray* that I will never forget what He has done for me. Oh, . . . please REMEMBER!"
- "I have made so many mistakes, so it's a source of comfort to me to know that through Christ's Atonement I can be made pure again."

Assignment

1. Where on this spectrum do you fall with regard to how open you are to change? Very | | | | | | | | | | | | Not at all

2. Make a list of those things in your life you would most like to change.

3. Is there a particular area of change that would be most helpful in helping to establish a loving relationship? What is that?

4. What can you do to enlist the Lord's help in modifying your behavior or overcoming what you have identified?

Section 2 Summary Points

1. What you sow in your youth, you will likely reap in your marriage.

2. It is more important to *be* the right one than it is to *find* the right one to marry.

3. There are five important areas of preparation on which you need to focus: physical, social, intellectual, emotional, and spiritual.

4. Unselfishness is one of the keys to a successful relationship.

5. The best way to prepare for a celestial marriage is to make the Lord your first priority.

6. Through the Atonement of Jesus Christ, you can make the needed changes in your life to become a successful candidate for marriage.

Understanding

LOVE

No man [or woman], however brilliant or well-informed, can . . . safely . . . dismiss . . . the wisdom of [lessons learned] in the laboratory of history. A youth boiling with hormones will wonder why he should not give full freedom to his sexual desires; [but] if he is unchecked by custom, morals, or laws, he may ruin his life before he . . . understand[s] that sex is a river of fire that must be banked and cooled by a hundred restraints if it is not to consume in chaos both the individual and the group" (Will and Ariel Durant, as quoted by Elder Jeffrey R. Holland, *Ensign*, November, 1998, 75).

CHAPTER 10

Love: Fact and Fiction

"Thou shalt live together in love"
(D&C 42:45).

Much of the happiness and unhappiness you will experience in mortality will be related to a powerful emotion—love. In the scripture quoted above, the Lord tells us that love is to characterize our relationships with each other. In the New Testament we are even told "God is love" (1 John 4:8). It is my belief that He wants all of us to experience love in its deepest and fullest sense. On the other hand, Satan seeks to prostitute and distort love—making of it something tawdry and destructive. Many young people have been deceived by the counterfeit descriptions of love that are evident all around us. Perhaps you have known people who one day announce they are "in love" and the next that they have "fallen out of love." You must be extremely careful also not to think of love as it is portrayed in the majority of TV sitcoms, movies, and romance novels. It has been said that there is a difference between Hollywood's "reel love" and "real love."

Nephi warned us that in the last days even some of the humble followers of Christ would "err because they are taught by the precepts of men" (2 Nephi 28:14). You must therefore be careful in your high school, college, and university classes. If you are not, you might be persuaded to buy into the false philosophies of the world about love.

Reflecting on Satan's great power to deceive, President Benson has said, "We must be aware."[1] The way to avoid deception is to get the facts. The truths about love are found in the standard works and the teachings of our latter-day prophets and apostles. This section will focus on what these truths are relating to love.

A myth is an unfounded or false notion about something. Given the powerful emotions that are involved, it is little wonder that a great many misconceptions and erroneous beliefs about love have found their way into our culture. Researchers have found that unrealistic expectations, false beliefs, and myths about love and marriage contribute greatly to "creating disappointment and dissatisfaction in marriage."[2] What this means to you is that believing these myths about love could negatively affect your future happiness. Jesus said that if we know the truth, the truth will make us free (see John 8:32). Free to what?

- Free to make correct choices.
- Free to see things as they really are.
- Free to avoid mistakes that could rob us of happiness.

Here are ten myths about love that are widely accepted in our world. Many of them are half-truths. Acceptance of any one of them could affect your future happiness in marriage:

1. Fiction: True love is love at first sight.

Fact: There is such a thing as attraction at first sight, but that is usually based mainly on physical appearance. Some people have known or felt they would marry a person after they first meet, but that is not necessarily love. Love involves commitment, respect, and trust, attributes of a relationship that develop over time. An initial attraction could be the beginning of love, but it takes time for love to grow and mature.

2. Fiction: When you can't think of anything but the person in whom you are interested, that means you are in love.

Fact: This is only partially true. Such a preoccupation may be the beginning of a loving relationship but is more likely to be characteristic of infatuation, a shallower emotion. As love matures, we learn to control our feelings.

3. *Fiction: Engaging in physical intimacy before marriage enhances a relationship and fosters love.*

Fact: Physical involvement before marriage puts stress on a relationship and makes it difficult to assess your true feelings. Couples who refrain from becoming physically intimate until after marriage and who keep the covenants they made at baptism have a greater chance of developing a deep friendship and an eternal love. Friendship is the key to a happy, enduring marriage. Engaging in premarital sex can fool people into thinking they are in love when they are really only lusting after each other.

4. *Fiction: Being somewhat dishonest with each other safeguards love.*

Fact: True love and friendship are based on honesty. "Playing games" with each other's emotions, hiding true feelings, or disguising our real self are immature ways to behave and do not contribute to a lasting relationship. Honesty builds trust, which is essential in a truly loving relationship.

5. *Fiction: If my partner really loved me, he or she would intuitively know what I want and need.*

Fact: Love does not give us the ability to read each other's minds. An honest and mature relationship depends on both parties honestly communicating their feelings, wants, and needs.

6. *Fiction: The strict moral guidelines that are part of the gospel stifle a relationship and are an impediment to true love.*

Fact: Satan would have you believe that the commandments have nothing to do with true love. That is absolutely false! The commandments to be chaste, to be honest, and to keep our covenants are the guardrails that protect us from making mistakes that destroy true love.

7. *Fiction: Being in love is a purely emotional rather than a rational experience.*

Fact: This is only half true. Though being in love can be a highly emotional experience, lasting love also involves an intellectual and spiritual commitment. Too many people blindly follow their feelings when they should also be using their heads.

8. *Fiction: A kiss is an indication of caring and possibly of love.*

Fact: This can be true but may not always be so. Many people kiss simply because it is fun, physically stimulating, or the expected thing to do. It may have nothing to do with love or even caring about the person.

9. *Fiction: Just because you date a nonmember of the Church doesn't mean you will marry one.*

Fact: This is a half-truth. Some people date nonmembers and don't marry outside the Church. But we fall in love with and marry those we date and "hang around with." The chances of a nonmember joining the Church after marriage are statistically very low.

10. *Fiction: When you are really in love, the intensity of the feeling is always high.*

Fact: Contrary to what is portrayed in the media, the intensity of loving feelings ebbs and flows, depending on a number of factors such as health, stress, and mood. The feeling of euphoria that is often involved is not constant. Some days we may not feel as "in love" as we do at other times. Love is a dynamic, growing, changing experience, and to keep it growing we must constantly work at it. Love, like a flower, needs nourishment.

Assignment

Consider for a moment where you obtained the notions you have about the nature of love.

- Are they based on sound understanding?

- Which of them are the product of romantic fantasies or portrayals in movies, books, or in music?

- Do you need to rethink some of your ideas?

- Which ones?

CHAPTER 11

Romantic Love

⌒🍂

*"Neither is the man without the woman,
neither the woman without the man, in the Lord"*
(1 Corinthians 11:11).

⌒🍂

Someone has written, "Love makes the world go round!" And our world is filled with songs, movies, and books about romantic love. Romantic love is one of the three essential elements of a mature, Godly love. But what is romantic love? Romantic love has to do with the desires and passions that motivate us to want to be physically close to a member of the opposite sex. Such love begins with an initial attraction, can grow into romance, and lead from there to courtship and marriage. Contrary to what many young people believe, the feelings associated with romantic love do not end with marriage and after the honeymoon! Married couples, even those who have been married for many years, continue to experience such feelings, which in fact can deepen as the years go by.

Elder Boyd K. Packer described this maturing of romantic love in these words: "Ideally, mating begins with romance. Though customs may vary, it flourishes with all the storybook feelings of excitement and anticipation, and sometimes rejection. There are moonlight and roses, love letters, love songs, poetry, the holding of hands and other worthy expressions of affection between a young man and a young woman. The world disappears around a couple, and they experience feelings of joy. Every couple in love is positive that no couple since Adam and Eve has felt quite the same as they do.

"There are other patterns of romance which appear to be too sensible, too quiet, even dull. Nevertheless, they embody the depth of affection and romantic love that deadly serious, silly senses, head-in-the-clouds-ones will experience only as they mature.

"And, if you suppose that the full-blown rapture of young romantic love is the sum of the possibilities which spring from the fountains of life, you have not yet lived to see the devotion and the comfort of longtime married love. Married couples are tried by temptation, misunderstandings, separation, financial problems, by family crises, by illness, and all the while love grows stronger. The mature love has a bliss not even imagined by newlyweds."[1]

Does what Elder Packer says seem peculiar to you? Do you think it is possible that romantic love continues to grow and mature after the marriage ceremony? Isn't that something to look forward to? President David O. McKay and his wife, Emma Ray, were famous in the Church for their love and their sometimes publicly displayed affection for each other. Even in their elderly years they were seen holding hands. Consider the tender feelings of romantic love in a poem President McKay wrote to Emma Ray on his ninetieth birthday:

> You say that I'm ninety, there must be some mistake,
> For throughout my body there is no pain or ache,
> It's true I respond less keenly to sound
> And forget where I put things as I strew them around.
> But it's no time at all since Tommy and I
> Took Nettie Belle and Annie [horses] our fortunes to try.
> At the "U," when seeking apartments where we could stay,
> I met for the first time a maiden called Ray.
> You say that I'm ninety, why she's still by my side,
> As precious and sweet as when as my bride
> In the springtime of life, with hearts all aglow
> We faced life together come wail or come woe.
> Family cares came heavy, but not a complaint.

> Forty-four children now praise her as saint.
> Companion, counselor, adviser always
> My wife for eternity, my own Emma Ray.

Three years later, President McKay was being pushed in his wheel-chair from his room in the Hotel Utah to the elevators by President N. Eldon Tanner. When they reached the elevators, President McKay said, "Oh, I'm sorry, we must go back." Without asking why, President Tanner immediately pushed him back to the apartment. "What was the problem? He hadn't kissed Emma Ray good-bye. He was then ninety-three."[2]

President Gordon B. Hinckley has also provided us a description of enduring romantic love.

"May I be personal for a moment? I sat at dinner across the table from my wife the other evening. It was fifty-five years ago that we were married in the Salt Lake Temple. The wondrous aura of young womanhood was upon her. She was beautiful, and I was bewitched. Now, for more than half a century, we have walked together through much of storm as well as sunshine. Today neither of us stands as tall as we once did. As I looked at her across the table, I noted a few wrinkles in her face and hands. But are they less beautiful than before? No, in fact, they are more so. Those wrinkles have a beauty of their own, and inherent in their very presence is something that speaks reassuringly of strength and integrity and a love that runs more deeply and quietly than ever before."[3]

Wouldn't it be wonderful to have an enduring love such as that experienced by President and Sister McKay and by President and Sister Hinckley? To achieve this, you must understand the relevance of romantic love from a gospel perspective. Elder Boyd K. Packer addressed this when he said, "Romantic love . . . is not only a part of life, but literally a dominating influence of it. It is deeply and significantly religious. There is no abundant life without it. Indeed, the highest degree of the Celestial Kingdom is unobtainable in the absence of it."[4]

Does such a statement about romantic love shock you? Have you ever thought of romance as being "significantly religious" or that "there is no abundant life without it"? If these concepts are foreign to you, it may be because of what you have seen in the movies, heard in the music of the day, been taught in school, or heard described in the locker room or at a party. For many people, romantic love is a passion that comes upon a person suddenly and cannot be controlled; a secretive thing to be snickered or giggled at; or sometimes something dirty and forbidden. To properly understand and enjoy romantic love, we must rethink the role of passion and sex and begin seeing these God-given gifts as components of the gospel of Jesus Christ and not the cornerstones of Satan's perverted doctrines. Indeed, the only way to understand these powerful emotions and keep them in check is in the context of the plan of happiness our Heavenly Father has designed for us.

In the New Testament, Paul counseled us to "put on the full armour of God" (Ephesians 6:11). The Apostle then went on to describe the various pieces of armor necessary to protect us from the fiery darts of the adversary. Each piece of armor was to protect an area that Satan would attack. The armor that covered the loins, or the reproductive area of our body, was truth. If you know the truth about romantic love, it will help you avoid Satan's attack on your virtue. Here are four truths taken from the standard works and Church leaders about this sacred power:

1. We lived with our Father in Heaven in a premortal life.

That we are spirit children of God, our Heavenly Father, is one of the most glorious truths of the Restoration. It was in our premortal life that we learned about his plan for our happiness. The ultimate goal of his plan is that we all might one day return to him and receive a fullness of joy in his kingdom.

2. God created this earth for us and gave us our physical body.

This earth was created as the place where we would learn, grow, and prove ourselves. We were given two wonderful gifts to accomplish this: a physical body and agency, or the right to choose for ourselves. This physical body would enable us to enjoy all the good experiences of life, including marriage and physical union with our mates. Through the proper use of this sacred power we would become partners with God in providing physical tabernacles for his spirit children. The gift of agency allows us to choose how we will utilize the sacred power of procreation—reverently and in keeping with the guidelines given to us by God, or carnally, in violation of God's law.

3. The God-given power to procreate is the very key to happiness in this life and in the eternities to come. Conversely, its misuse leads to sorrow and condemnation.

The way we view and use the power of procreation is a major part of the test we are undergoing in mortality. If we perceive sexuality to be evil and dirty, as portrayed by some comedians and television talk show hosts, it will adversely affect how we relate to those we date and the one we will eventually marry. Elder Hugh B. Brown addressed this topic when he wrote: "Many [LDS] marriages have been wrecked on the dangerous rocks of ignorant and debased sex behavior, both before and after marriage. Gross ignorance on the part of newlyweds on the subject of the proper place and functioning of sex results in much unhappiness and many broken homes.

"Thousands of young people come to the marriage altar almost illiterate insofar as this basic fundamental function is concerned."[5]

The scriptures and our Church leaders teach that this power, rather than being evil, is good when kept within the bounds the Lord has set. After creating Adam, the Lord said, "It is not good that man should be alone; I will make him an help meet for him" (Genesis 2:18). The term *help meet* means his complement, or other half. After Eve was created, Adam said, "Therefore shall a man leave his father and his mother, and shall cleave unto his wife: and they shall be one flesh" (Genesis 2:24). The term *one flesh* refers to physical union and to their sharing the power of procreation. Speaking of this power, President Spencer W. Kimball taught that physical intimacy between husband and wife was planned for in the premortal life: "When the Lord organized his world and established his policies, he could have filled the earth with physical bodies in some other way than that which he designed. [His plan] required both a man and a woman to reproduce through sexual relations and to also care for, rear, and teach the child gospel truths once he/she was born. This process of reproduction was designed before this world was organized."[6]

Clearly, romantic love and physical intimacy in marriage are ordained of God as part of His eternal plan. Elder Parley P. Pratt, a member of the original Quorum of the Twelve Apostles, wrote, "When God made man, male and female; he planted in their bosoms those affections which are calculated to promote their happiness and union."[7] Elder Boyd K. Packer has also testified, "I want to tell you young people that this power within you is good. It is a gift from God our Father. In the righteous exercise of it as in nothing else, we may come close to him."[8]

4. Romantic love serves at least four major purposes.

When we view this sacred power from the perspective of the plan of happiness, we can understand its major purposes. First, this power encourages men and women to pursue each other that they might find a companion. This is most often accomplished through dating, courtship, and marriage.

Second, sexual union is the means by which children are brought into this world. President Spencer W. Kimball has emphasized, "The Bible celebrates sex and its proper use, presenting it as God-created, God-ordained, God-blessed. It makes plain that God himself implanted the physical magnetism between the sexes for two reasons: for the propagation of the human race, and for the expression of that kind of love between man and wife that makes for true oneness. His command to the first man and woman to be 'one flesh' was as important as his command to 'be fruitful and multiply.'"[9]

Third, this gift from God is a means of fostering love between a man and a woman who are married. Our Church leaders have continually affirmed that sexual relations within marriage are divinely approved, not only for the purpose of procreation but as a means of expressing love and strengthening the emotional and spiritual union between husband and wife.

And fourth, a strong, appropriate sexual bond between husband and wife is a powerful aid in helping them remain faithful to each other.

Romantic love is, as you can see, not just a part of the plan of happiness; it is a key element. It is a vital part of the glue that holds a married couple together, providing for them a very private and intimate experience that they share with each other and no one else. It is good, and it is a gift from God to us. Those who learn here in mortality to keep romantic love within the bounds the Lord has set will enjoy the blessings of eternal companionship as well as eternal increase in the highest degree of the celestial kingdom (see D&C 131:1–4).

Assignment

The following questions are based on the information in this chapter.

- Are you grateful for your physical body? Do you view it as sacred?

- Do you appreciate the fact that you are a man or a woman?

- Are you grateful to your Heavenly Father that you have a desire to marry and to enjoy a full and rich companionship with your spouse?

- How do you feel about the potential of having children? Are you prepared to provide for them a loving, righteous environment in which they can grow up in safety, love, and the light of the gospel?

- Do you have some inappropriate attitudes about sexuality and intimacy that you need to change? In light of the sacred nature of sex, does anything in your behavior toward members of the opposite sex need to be modified in some way?

- Are you determined to keep romantic love within the bounds the Lord has set? What standards have you set for yourself in your dating and courtship activities?

CHAPTER 12

Satan's Half-Truths about Romantic Love

◦❦◦

"Satan hath sought to deceive you"
(D&C 50:3).

◦❦◦

Satan has been referred to as the great deceiver, and there is no area he would rather deceive you than in the area of love. Elder Boyd K. Packer has warned, "The single purpose of Lucifer is to oppose the great plan of happiness, to corrupt the purest, most beautiful and appealing experiences of life: romance, love, marriage, and parenthood."[1]

Why is Satan so concerned about love, marriage, and parenthood? One possible answer is that he will never have a physical body and will never, ever experience the happiness and joy associated with the powers of procreation. And he "seeketh that all men might be miserable like unto himself" (2 Nephi 2:27).

How does he encourage young people to misuse this power? He is too subtle to come out and openly invite you to be immoral. He will not make sin look black, for that would be too easy for you to detect. Rather, he will take some truth and shade it with a little gray. Once you have accepted this, he will add a little more gray, until what you said you would never do, you have done. President Kimball has provided us this warning: "The adversary is subtle; he is cunning, he knows that he cannot induce good men and women immediately to do major evils so he moves slyly, whispering half truths until he has his intended victims following him, and finally he clamps his chains upon them and fetters them tight, and then he laughs at their discomfiture and their misery."[2]

A half-truth is a statement that contains some truth but also a lie. With regard to love and marriage, you cannot allow yourself to be deceived. Such decisions and mistakes will have eternal significance. What, then, are the half-truths Satan employs when it comes to romantic love?

Half-Truth 1: Physical intimacy before marriage will enhance and strengthen the love a couple has for one another.

Truth: Physical intimacy *does* enhance a relationship and strengthen the bond between a man and a woman but not outside marriage. The feelings of guilt and shame and the unworthiness that result from engaging in premarital sex are destructive. Alma's declaration remains true: "Wickedness never was happiness" (Alma 41:10).

Lie: You are permitted to do this before marriage as long as you're in love.

Should you believe this half-truth, you could be deceived into thinking that you are in love when in reality you are, as President Spencer W. Kimball has said, merely "in lust." He further explained, "When the unmarried yield to the lust that induces intimacies and indulgence, they have permitted the body to dominate and have placed the spirit in chains. It is unthinkable that anyone could call this love."[3]

Elder Boyd K. Packer has said: "The greatest deception foisted upon the human race in our day is that overemphasis of physical gratification as it is related to romantic love. It is merely a repetition of the same delusion that has been impressed on every generation in ages past. When we learn that physical gratification is only incident to, and not the compelling force of love itself, we have made a supreme discovery. If only physical gratification should interest you, you need not be selective at all. This power is possessed by almost everyone. Alone, without attendant love, this relationship becomes nothing—indeed, less and worse than nothing."[4]

Dr. William E. Hartman, a member of the Church and a noted sociologist, said, "I have seen personal intimacy do more to destroy intelligent mate selection, and reflect immaturity on the part of young Latter-day Saints, than any other one thing I could mention."[5]

The reason for this is that romantic love is such a powerful force that it can become the focus of the relationship. "Kissing," says Rene Yasenekis, "is a means of getting two people so close together that they can't see anything wrong with each other."[6] And that's exactly what happens! The initial rush of romance is not enough to sustain a marriage for the duration of life, let alone eternity. A relationship built on the teachings of the Lord might ideally develop as follows:

This type of relationship is built on a solid foundation. When the problems of marriage come, the couple is better able to deal with them because of the foundation of friendship and commitment they have already established. Note the difference when this order is reversed.

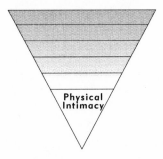

This relationship is built on a very unstable foundation. No wonder in today's world, where premature physical intimacy is the basis of so many relationships, there are so many divorces! Too many are "in like"

because of physical attraction but are not really "in love." The type of love that includes all three dimensions lasts forever; it is eternal.

What are the consequences of engaging in sexual behavior before marriage?

- When sex becomes the main focus of the relationship, it takes the place of exchanging ideas, having legitimate fun, learning to appreciate the other's personality, and sharing spiritual experiences, all to the detriment of the relationship.
- Each person loses sight of his or her long-term, spiritual objectives.
- Mutual trust and respect are destroyed, which often causes the parties to lose interest in each other, if not resent the other for what has been lost.
- Feelings of guilt drive away the Spirit of the Lord.
- The couple gradually become numb to their behavior. In a real sense, they dull their consciences.
- They lose the ability to think clearly and objectively.
- They surrender the privilege of being married in the temple.

President Kimball asked young people who are involved in inappropriate and immoral behavior to consider the following: "If anyone feels that petting or other deviations are demonstrations of love, let him ask himself: 'If this beautiful body that I have misused suddenly became deformed, or paralyzed, would my reactions be the same? If this lovely face were scarred by flames, or this body that I have used were to suddenly become rigid, would there still be love?' Answers to these questions might test one to see if he really is in love or if it is only physical attraction that has encouraged the improper physical contacts."[7]

Half-Truth 2: You can remain virtuous as long as you don't go all the way.

Truth: The Lord desires that we be pure and virtuous.

Lie: Petting and other types of sexual behavior do not constitute immorality; so long as we don't engage in sexual intercourse, we have not gone too far.

Many young people rationalize their behavior by refusing to believe that there are appropriate and inappropriate ways of expressing affection prior to marriage. Appropriate affection includes holding hands and exchanging an occasional hug or friendship kiss. However, when couples go beyond this, engaging in necking, French kissing, and caressing private parts of the body, they awaken passions that are difficult to control and often lead to fornication. President Spencer W. Kimball condemned the "soul kiss" (French kiss) as "an abomination [that] stirs passions to the eventual loss of virtue. Even if timely courtship justifies the kiss it should be a clean, decent, sexless one."[8] He further taught, "Kissing has been prostituted and has degenerated to develop and express lust instead of affection, honor, and admiration. To kiss in casual dating is asking for trouble. What do kisses mean when given out like pretzels and robbed of sacredness?"[9]

Elder Mark E. Petersen of the Quorum of the Twelve stated that a kiss is a sign of affection, a pledge of love and loyalty.[10]

Why do you suppose prophets of God have counseled you to keep a kiss sacred? What is so dangerous about kissing? The passions aroused by prolonged kissing stimulate desires that can lead you into a situation where you might do things you never considered doing otherwise.

There is another reason to be very careful about kissing. Many of my students have told me that when kissing starts, talking stops. That is, necking or making out introduces an element in the relationship that gives greater priority to physical gratification than the building of friendship and trust. In today's world, it requires great courage to accept and live the standards taught by Church leaders relative to kissing. Many young people dismiss such counsel, contending it doesn't apply to them or believing that such advice is outdated—the product of narrow thinking.

To maintain such a standard also requires a strong testimony that, as the prophets of God have said, the powers of procreation are sacred. One young man witnessed such courage and testimony as he stood at the doorstep with his date. He asked if he could kiss her goodnight. She looked at him from behind the screen door and said,

"A kiss is special to me. When you marry, won't you want to marry a girl who has reserved herself for you?"

"Sure, I suppose every young man wants to marry a pure girl," he replied.

Then his date said, "And shouldn't you be just as pure as she is?"

This young man learned a great lesson that night as a young Latter-day Saint woman taught him something about the sacredness of a kiss.

You must decide where to draw the line in sharing your affection. Most young people who have crossed the line and committed an immoral act have found that, lacking clear boundaries, they reached a point where they were powerless to say "no."

Half-Truth 3: You can think and look all you want as long as you don't touch.

Truth: Sexual arousal is fired through seeing and thinking.

Lie: It is okay to think lustful thoughts.

Thoughts trigger actions. Satan knows this, and so he tells us that we can think whatever we want. He takes advantage of our ignorance about how our body functions and tempts us where we are weak—in our minds. This is how it works: we see something, which leads us to think about it; the thought leads to a feeling, and feeling leads to action. Our Heavenly Father knows this. After all, he created us. And to protect us, he has provided an "owner's manual." This manual is found in the standard works and in the teachings of Church leaders. Note what they say about our thoughts:

"As [a man] thinketh in his heart, so is he" (Proverb 23:7).

"Whosoever looketh on a woman, to lust after her, hath committed adultery already in his heart" (3 Nephi 12:28).

"Let virtue garnish thy thoughts unceasingly" (D&C 121:45).

One of the most tragic stories in the Old Testament is that of King David, who in his youth showed so much promise but who fell victim to his unbridled passions. Consider where his thoughts led him. His story is found in 2 Samuel, chapter 11, where we are told:

- David took a walk one night on the roof of his palace in Jerusalem.
- From that vantage point, he saw a woman washing herself. Rather than avert his eyes, he lusted after her.
- Bathsheba was the wife of another man, and David himself was married; nevertheless, the king sent for her, inviting her to his palace.
- They succumbed to their passions and committed adultery, resulting in Bathsheba's becoming pregnant with King David's child.
- David plotted to hide their sin and eventually arranged for Bathsheba's husband, Uriah, to be killed in battle—essentially murdering him.
- With Uriah out of the way, David married Bathsheba.

It is difficult to imagine more sinful behavior, and we are told that as a consequence of his transgressions, David forfeited his chance for exaltation (see D&C 132:39).

We might ask ourselves at what point did David fall into the web of desire? Was there a time when he could have halted his descent and avoided the sins of which he was ultimately guilty? Isn't it clear that the tragedy began when, looking upon Bathsheba, he began to entertain lustful thoughts?

Sometimes, like David, young people do not recognize the impact of their thoughts. Elder Boyd K. Packer emphasized the power of thoughts to shape our actions when he said, "The mind is a stage." He went on to counsel us to rid ourselves of unworthy thoughts by memorizing the words of a favorite hymn and recalling them to help push unworthy thoughts out of our minds.[11]

President Gordon B. Hinckley illustrated the importance of switching our thoughts by relating an experience he had while working for a railroad company. One day he received a call from New Jersey that a passenger train had arrived without the baggage car. "We discovered that the train had been properly made up in Oakland, California, and properly delivered to St. Louis. . . . But in the St. Louis yards, a thoughtless switchman had moved a piece of steel just three inches. That piece of steel was a switch point, and the car that should have been in Newark, New Jersey, was in New Orleans, Louisiana, thirteen hundred miles away."[12]

At what point should David have switched tracks, switched his thoughts? If he had done so, how might his tragic life have ended differently? When we follow the Lord's manual and control our thoughts, we receive ultimate joy and happiness.

Half-Truth 4: Sex is natural and pleasurable, so why not enjoy it?

Truth: Sex *is* natural and pleasurable. God made it that way for a purpose—to ensure the perpetuation of humankind and to enhance and strengthen the union between marriage partners.

Lie: Sex should be given full expression, regardless of our marital status.

Our sexuality is God-given, and sex is not of itself dirty or sinful. What is sinful is the sharing of this sacred and precious gift with anyone other than your lawfully wedded spouse. Authorization to use these sacred powers is limited to those who have been lawfully married and who have pledged to each other strict fidelity. Within the bonds of marriage, sexual relations serve to strengthen commitment and provide a closeness that only such intimacy can provide. On the other hand, those who engage in unmarried, recreational sex are in violation of God's law and will reap the bitter consequences.

Half-Truth 5: Because we are physically attracted to each other, we are necessarily in love.

Truth: Physical attraction is a dimension of true love.

Lie: Physical attraction is the *most important* dimension of love.

We have already seen that romantic love is an essential and vital component in a successful marriage. But remember, there are at least two other dimensions that are important—friendship and godliness. Elder Neal A. Maxwell has warned, "The adversary, interestingly enough, has even tried to ruin the word *love* itself, making it seem to be a one dimensional thing, a basic act instead of a grand thing."[13]

A growing, mature love will have much more than just a romantic dimension.

Half-Truth 6: Repenting of a sexual transgression is relatively easy.

Truth: Through repentance we can be forgiven of a moral transgression.

Lie: Repentance is easy.

Too often, young people fail to recognize the seriousness of sexual transgressions, assuming that such sin is trivial and forgiveness is easily obtained. Though it is possible to repent and obtain complete forgiveness for the misuse of these sacred powers, the process is *not* easy! President Spencer W. Kimball taught "one is not repentant until he bares his soul and admits his actions without excuses or rationalizations, until he has really and truly suffered. Suffering is a very important part of repentance. One has not begun to repent until he has suffered intensely for his sins."[14]

Repentance of sexual transgressions involves recognizing the seriousness of the sin, confessing to one's bishop, sincerely pleading with the Lord for forgiveness, and making a commitment not to misuse this power again. Depending on the seriousness of the transgression, gaining forgiveness may require the individual to undergo disciplinary action, which may result in the loss of the right to partake of the sacrament, speak or pray in Church meetings, or have a calling. The road to forgiveness can be walked if one is truly sorrowful for what he or she has done, but we should never assume that it is an easy thing to do. Many a young person has sat tearfully before his or her bishop, wishing with all their heart they had used better judgment, listened to the counsel of their parents and Church leaders, and avoided the temptations that led to their downfall.

If your virtue is that precious, how can you protect it? The story of Joseph in the Old Testament provides a dramatic contrast to the story of King David. Employed as a trusted servant in the home of a man named Potiphar, Joseph was lusted after by Potipher's wife, who propositioned the young Israelite "day by day." Finally she became so determined that she grabbed him by his clothing and demanded, "Lie with me." Joseph had clear standards. He had made a covenant with the Lord to safeguard his virtue. The scriptural account says, "He left his garment in her hand, and fled, and got him out" (Genesis 39:7–12).

Though Joseph's heroic, virtuous decision was not immediately rewarded, the Lord eventually blessed him beyond Joseph's ability to imagine. And thousands of years later, we remember him for his integrity and moral courage. Contrast that to David, who, though he was a king, must forever sorrow over the transgression that cost him his eternal life. How different his story might have been if after catching a glimpse of Bathsheba, he had "got himself out"! Instead, he learned a bitter lesson: violating the law of chastity destroys one's soul.

Like Joseph, you must set clear standards. Develop a plan, a set of rules that will help you stay virtuous.

Elder Hartman Rector Jr. spent twenty-six years as a Navy pilot and used that experience to make an interesting analogy: "Let's pretend that the navy had a commandment—'Thou shalt not fly thy airplane in the trees.' As a matter of fact, they did have such a commandment. In order to really be free of the commandment, it becomes necessary for me to add a commandment of my own to the Navy's commandment, such as, 'Thou shalt not fly thy airplane closer than 5,000 feet to the trees.' When you do this, you make the Navy's commandment of not flying in the trees easy to live, and the safety factor is tremendously increased."[15]

The same principle will help you protect your virtue. It is not enough to say, "I will not have sex before I am married." To succeed in keeping that commitment, you must set strict rules for yourself! Rules that will keep you well away from the dangers of sexual transgression. Here are some rules set by some young people I have known:

- Always double date.
- Never lie down with someone of the opposite sex, even to watch television.
- Never look at pornography or watch R-rated or PG-13 movies that contain questionable scenes.

- Never go into a bedroom with a member of the opposite sex.
- Do not stay out past 1:00 A.M. on a date.
- Do not wear immodest or provocative clothing.
- Do not share passionate kisses with anyone but your married companion.

Do these rules seem prudish or even stupid to you? Ask anyone who has been guilty of a sexual transgression, and you will find they broke one or several of these rules on the way to their downfall. You need not accept Satan's half-truths. Happiness now and in eternity is worth planning and waiting for. Why take the chance of jeopardizing true future happiness for a few moments of pleasure?

A segment from the television program *Sesame Street* illustrates how some people sacrifice the things that matter most for those that matter least. In this segment, Cookie Monster has won a prize on a quiz show.

"What a moment it was! After Mrs. Monster joined her spouse on the stage, the emcee congratulated the couple and offered them their choice among three big prizes—a $200,000 dream home next month, a $20,000 new car next week, or a cookie right now. Mr. and Mrs. Monster furrowed their furry brows and carefully weighed the pros and cons. As the timer buzzed, a big smile broke across Mr. Monster's face, and he greedily announced 'Cookie!'"[16]

This reminds us of Esau, who, because he was hungry, was willing to trade his birthright and eternal blessings for a mess of pottage (see Genesis 25:23–34). Many blessings and great happiness await those who have the conviction and the courage to, as Alma counseled his son Shiblon, "bridle" their passions (see Alma 38:12):

- The blessing of the companionship of the Holy Ghost
- The blessing of a clear conscience
- The blessing of respect from those we date and with whom we associate
- The blessing of an unsullied reputation
- The blessing of knowing we are valued for attributes other than just physical
- The blessing of being worthy to go to the temple

Assignment

In 1995, the First Presidency and Quorum of the Twelve Apostles published a powerful document called *The Family: A Proclamation to the World*. Among the truths in that inspired declaration are the following. As you read these, reflect on Satan's half-truths and the lies that are accepted in the world about sexuality, marriage, and the role of parents.

The Family: A Proclamation to the World

1. The first commandment that God gave to Adam and Eve pertained to their potential for parenthood as husband and wife. We declare that God's commandment for His children to multiply and replenish the earth remains in force. We further declare that God has commanded that the sacred powers of procreation are to be employed only between man and woman, lawfully wedded as husband and wife.

2. We declare the means by which mortal life is created to be divinely appointed. We affirm the sanctity of life and its importance in God's eternal plan.

3. The family is ordained of God. Marriage between man and woman is essential to His eternal plan. . . . Children are entitled to birth within the bonds of matrimony, and to be reared by a father and a mother who honor marital vows with complete fidelity.

CHAPTER 13

Friendship Love

"A friend loveth at all times"
(Proverb 17:17).

Elder Marion D. Hanks told the following experience: "As I walked up the aisle in the auditorium at a university recently, I stopped and said to a young man sitting on the end of the row, 'Who is that beautiful girl sitting by you?' 'My best friend,' he said, right off the top of his head. 'Oh, and is she also your wife?' 'Yes.' I spoke to her, 'Is that true? Are you his best friend?' 'Yes.' 'And is he your best friend?' 'Yes.' 'Do you know how lucky you two are to be married to your sweetheart who is also your best friend?' They said, 'We know.'"[1]

Someone once said, "Become friends before you become sweethearts." The love of friendship is much more than physical attraction, which is usually only "skin deep." A marriage based on a solid friendship has a much greater chance of enduring the problems and stresses of life. A twenty-five-year study on marriage found that the most important ingredient in a lasting marriage is friendship.[2]

I am very thankful that I married my best friend, Susan. Our friendship has grown and matured over the years of our marriage and has in many ways become the most satisfying element in our relationship. President Spencer W. Kimball has indicated why a friendship is so important in marriage:

"While one is young and well and strong and beautiful or handsome and attractive, he or she can (for the moment) almost name the price and write the ticket; but the time comes when these temporary things have had their day; when wrinkles come and aching joints; when hair is thin and bodies bulge; when nerves are frayed and tempers are taut; when wealth is dissipated; . . .

"There comes a time when those who flattered us and those whose wit and charm deceived us may leave us to our fate. Those are times when we want friends, good friends, common friends, loved ones, tied with immortal bonds—people who will nurse our illnesses, tolerate our eccentricities, and love us with pure, undefiled affection. Then we need an unspoiled companion who will not count our wrinkles, remember our stupidities nor remember our weaknesses; then is when we need a loving companion with whom we have suffered and wept and prayed and worshipped; one with whom we have suffered sorrow and disappointments, one who loves us for what we are or intend to be rather than what we appear to be in our gilded shell."[3]

Building a satisfying marriage requires great cooperation, and friendship is one of the most important elements in a happy relationship. One thing that will prepare you for marriage is for you to learn how to make and keep friends. People who do not learn how to get along with others and make some friends before marriage will likely find it difficult to make a friend out of a husband or a wife. The stages in a developing relationship can be diagrammed as follows:

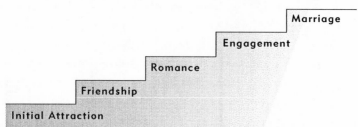

Our society places great emphasis on physical attraction. So much so, that for many this is the major consideration in looking for a companion. While physical attraction is important, it should not be the major criterion. By this I am not trying to say that physical attraction is not important. As discussed in the chapter on romantic love, it is very important that you be physically attracted to the one you marry. On this topic Elder Marion D. Hanks has said: "Married people are sweethearts in a special creative union, blessed with a powerful chemistry that draws them together. The sexual union . . . is one of the many unions or unities in marriage [and] is critical and significant, a divinely bestowed blessing."[4]

But we must also keep in mind the counsel the Lord gave to Samuel when the prophet was sent to choose a king from among the impressive-looking sons of Jesse: "Look not on his countenance, or on the height of his stature; . . . for the Lord seeth not as man seeth; for man looketh on the outward appearance, but the Lord looketh on the heart" (1 Samuel 16:7).

When choosing an eternal companion, what is on the inside is as important, if not more so, than what is on the outside. Not many relationships progress from friendship to romance. It has been estimated that 80 percent of the time people do not marry the first person they fall in love with.

Wouldn't it take some of the pressure off dating if your focus was trying to make friends with the people you date rather than worrying about whether or not you will become sweethearts? I tell my students that the better friend they become to others, the better the chance of their moving toward and building a happy marriage.

So, how do we learn to become a good friend and to develop strong friendships? I have asked my students to suggest what qualities make for a good friendship. Their answers have included the following: being honest, having similar interests, being dependable, knowing how to communicate, and being worthy of respect, trust, and loyalty. These qualities could be diagrammed as follows, with each quality being essential in a lasting friendship:

True friendship must be built on a foundation of honesty and chastity.

Chastity was discussed in chapters 11 and 12. Along with chastity, honesty is one of the most important building-blocks of a lasting friendship. Bishop Victor L. Brown said that this quality of honesty is one of "the basic virtues of a noble character."[5] But in today's world it is not uncommon for people to "play games" in their dating relationships. "Playing games" is an attempt to make another person think we are different from what we really are. Jesus referred to this in the scriptures as hypocrisy. One young woman related this experience:

"I returned to my apartment after a date, and my roommates asked me how it had gone. I told them I had a great time and mentioned that I had told my date how much I had enjoyed it. Their response was, 'Oh, you shouldn't have told him you had a good time. Keep him guessing. Never share how you really feel!'"

In many circles, this kind of thing is part of the dating "game." And one of the frustrating things for many young women, but young men too, is the number of others who will do or say anything to impress the one they are dating. Here are some areas where young people are often dishonest:

- Their attitude toward the Church
- Their expectations of each other
- Their goals in life
- Their past sins
- Their real feelings about a relationship or a person
- Their reasons for kissing

Why are people dishonest? Usually it is because they are afraid that if they tell the truth, others will not find them attractive. They fear being rejected. Therefore, to impress people, they portray themselves as something they are not. When people do not feel good about themselves, they either do not reveal their real feelings or they lie about them. Without honesty, a solid, enduring relationship can never be established. Honesty builds respect and trust, which are critical elements of a friendship. President Gordon B. Hinckley has said, "Where there is honesty, other virtues will follow."[6] And President David O. McKay affirmed:

"Honesty and sincerity are the basic virtues of a noble character. Honesty . . . is the first virtue mentioned in the thirteenth Article of Faith. It is founded on the first principles of human society and is the foundation principle of moral manhood. *It is impossible to associate manhood with dishonesty.* To be just with one's self and to others, one must be honest with himself and with others. This means honesty in speech as well as in actions. It means to avoid telling half truths as well as untruths."[7]

One area where young people are often the most dishonest is in the sharing of physical affection. Writing during the time that he was serving as president of Ricks College, Elder Bruce C. Hafen provided this counsel:

"During the time of courtship, always be emotionally honest in the expression of affection. Sometimes you are not as careful as you might be about when, how, and to whom you express your feelings of affection. You must realize that the desire to express affection can be motivated by things other than true love. . . . In short, one might simply say: save your kisses—you might need them some day. And when any of you—men or women—are given entrance to the heart of a trusting young friend, you stand on holy ground. In such a place you must be honest with yourself—and with your friend—about love and the expression of its symbols."[8]

Some young people have wondered if it is wise or even necessary to be totally honest in a relationship. They wonder if they should express every thought or opinion they have. If being "totally honest" means avoiding being deceitful, then the answer is certainly "yes." However, in order to spare a friend unnecessary pain, we often "bite our tongues" and avoid saying something that is hurtful, even if that thing is true. For example, if someone made a negative comment about one of our friends, we would certainly not want to pass it on for risk of hurting our friend's feelings. It is true that some things are better left unsaid. Being critical and judgmental with a friend, even though we are being honest with our feelings, never builds friendships.

When deciding what to say, remember to use the THINK method:
Is it **T**rue?
Is it **H**elpful?
Is it **I**mportant?
Is it **N**ecessary?
Is it **K**ind?

Dr. David Gardner, a former president of the University of Utah and then of the University of California, was once asked how, as a Mormon, he was able to have such good relations with so many diverse groups. He answered, "You have to decide what your own value system is and always be faithful to it."⁹ This is wonderful counsel for marriage preparation, for when you are honest and truthful you won't have to worry about impressing others or changing behavior later in a relationship.

Give yourselves time to know each other and your relationship time to develop.

I become very concerned when I hear about young people who agree to marry after knowing each other for only a month or two. I am certain there are cases where this has worked and the couple has had a successful marriage. However, in many instances it simply does not work. It takes time to build a friendship. Most often, when a relationship blossoms very quickly, it is because physical attraction and intimacy have become the focus of the relationship. How much time does it take to form a solid friendship? We need enough time to really get to know another person. That means seeing them in a variety of settings, not just on formal dates—in their home, around their parents and siblings, at their place of employment, on outings with other people, in recreational settings, and at church. Time to see them at their best and at their worst. Time to witness both positive and negative patterns of behavior.

I know a couple who had been acquainted since they were in the sixth grade and who had dated, off and on, through high school and college. Over those years, they had spent countless hours together in all kinds of settings. The young woman had even taken vacations with the young man's family while he was on his mission. They corresponded for the two years he was away, and they married shortly after he returned home.

After all that, the bride confessed that for a time after they were married it was like waking up with a stranger. There were so many things she didn't know about his personal habits, his personality, the foods he liked and didn't like, the way he organized his clothes and belongings, his preferences, and his way of thinking and doing things. For example, they had often gone dancing during their courtship. She enjoyed dancing and just assumed that it would remain a shared interest. She was surprised after their marriage (as many women are) to learn that he didn't enjoy dancing all that much but had gone dancing with her in an effort to impress her. Only after they were married did he express his true feelings.

Discovering these things is part of the excitement of being married, but discovering these things is also part of the challenge of learning to live with your spouse. Imagine the difficulty people experience when they marry after only a brief courtship, without having had the time to get to know each other at all.

There is something else I have learned in talking with many couples: it is much easier to make changes in a relationship or in yourself *before* marriage than *after* marriage. Why? There are at least three reasons:

First, after marriage the motivation to change is not as great because both husband and wife get quickly involved in the everyday business of life. Another factor is that before marriage, they usually take an interest in finding out about each other; but after settling into the routine of married life, there are many demands on them, and many couples complain that it is difficult to find time to spend together. This is particularly true when either or both are still in school and perhaps working as well or when children come along.

Second, during the dating and courtship stages, couples have eyes only for each other, and, wishing to impress each other, the two are likely to be on their best behavior. Once they are married, they become more relaxed and inevitably begin to take each other somewhat for granted. When this happens, little change occurs.

Third, after marriage we are more vulnerable to being hurt. Our self-esteem is more on the line because our mate sees us in every imaginable situation. It is not unusual for partners in a new marriage to become overly sensitive to criticism and to construct walls to protect their feelings. Pride then gets in the way and becomes an impediment to change.

The message? It is easier to make basic changes in yourself before marriage than it is after marriage! If you doubt that, find a newly wedded couple who is likely to give you a straight answer, and ask about the adjustments they have had to make.

The bottom line is: the more you learn about the one you love before you get married, the better. President David O. McKay put it this way, "During courtship keep your eyes wide open, but after marriage keep them half shut!"[10]

Communication and kindness are important.

One of the key factors in a friendship is that each person feels that the other person really cares. Looking back on your life, who do you feel really cared about you? What did they do that made you feel they cared about you? In most cases, you will find you had an open communication with each other. You could talk about anything and everything. Learning to express that interest to another individual is, according to Dr. Brent Barlow, "the single most important thing you can learn to do to become skilled at communication."[11]

Researchers at BYU found that couples "who were most satisfied with their marriages tended to spend their free time together in activities that allowed them to have lots of interaction and communication with each other."[12] They further found that equally important as the amount of time couples spent together was how much they communicated with each other.

Other research conducted at BYU found that as important as communication skills are in marriage, the kindness in the way people communicate may be even more important. "Masterful communication, without kindness, becomes masterful manipulation, and that unkindness in combination with high communication skills is frequently an act of verbal violence. Regardless of whether a couple is skilled or fumbles awkwardly in attempts to communicate, the feelings of kindness or unkindness behind the attempts seemed to come through in ways that matter."[13]

What does this mean to you? To have good relationships you do not need a master's degree in communications. What you do need is a kind and tender heart. It probably would not surprise you that one of the things that destroys friendships the quickest is anger. President David O. McKay is quoted as saying, "I'm going to tell you the most important secret of human life. The most critical need of the human soul is to be kind."[14]

Elder L. Lionel Kendrick has said, "There are certain kinds of un-Christlike communications which destroy relationships."[15] The following chart contrasts Christlike with un-Christlike communication:

Christlike	Un-Christlike
Kind	Often angry
Full of compassion	Full of contention
Truthful	Tells lies
Quick to forgive	Overly critical

If there are frequent expressions of anger and unkind behavior on the part of the person you are dating, it ought to be a red flag signaling that you had better carefully consider if there is any future in such a relationship.

Cultivate common interests and values.

One of the things that attracts us to other people is having common interests. When you think about the friends you have had, you'll likely discover that most of them like, enjoy, and believe the same things you do. Some such important interests and values are:

Interests	Values
Athletics	Religious/Spiritual
Hobbies	Family
Culture	Political

During my college days, I was assigned to be a home teacher to a newly married couple. For the life of me, I couldn't figure out how they had gotten together. The two had little to nothing in common, and they were always in conflict.

He liked sports—she disliked them.

He liked to watch TV—she didn't.

She liked to play table games—he didn't.

He had his friends—she had hers.

She enjoyed church—he didn't.

She wanted children—he didn't.

The only interest they shared was physical intimacy. That simply wasn't enough to hold the marriage together, and they eventually divorced. It occurred to me that if they had spent more time during their dating time learning about each other, they may not have even married.

I heard of one young man who said, "I want to marry a girl who is the exact opposite of me so that after our marriage we will have spice and variety in our relationship." A friend who had been married for years replied, "Marry someone who is the most like you, and I guarantee you that after you are married you will find enough differences to add spice and variety to your marriage." What did he mean by "someone who is the most like you"? Someone who holds the same values and who is similar in age, education, socioeconomic background, and religion. The more alike you are in these and other important areas, the greater the chance you can make the marriage work.

Dependability

It is difficult to remain friends with undependable people. Real friends do what they say they will do; they build confidence and trust because they can be depended on. When I asked my students to contrast the two types of behavior, here is what they said:

Dependable	Undependable
They are on time for appointments.	They are often late or sometimes do not even show up.
They call when they will be late.	They never call when they will be late.

| They follow through with what they say they will do. | They always have excuses for why they didn't do something. |

A sense of humor and cheerfulness are essential.

A sense of humor is like the oil in a car engine—it eases the friction. There are situations that arise in all friendships that create tension or stress, and we all experience moments when we are somewhat down or discouraged. A sense of humor can help us survive such moments and work our way through our problems.

Some people have a knack for finding humor in what appear to be bleak situations; however, there are some types of humor that are not endearing but are in fact destructive. For example, some people use sarcasm to put people down in a supposedly humorous way. People usually do not like to be the brunt of a joke, and making fun of a friend in front of others can be hurtful. Teasing is another negative use of humor. There are those who take teasing personally. Those who consistently have fun at the expense of others may have a sadistic streak in them. Though a sense of humor is important, we need to be careful about taking it to extremes.

President David O. McKay counseled us to be cheerful: "It is our duty to seek to acquire the art of being cheerful. It will hold in check the demons of despair and stifle the power of discouragement and hopelessness."[16] I have found in my own life that I can *choose* to be cheerful or moody. It is extremely difficult to be around moody people. Should you have this tendency, take President McKay's advice and seek to be cheerful.

Bishop Glenn L. Pace has said, "While the gospel is sacred and serious, sometimes we take ourselves a little too seriously. A sense of humor, especially about ourselves, is an attribute worthy of development."[17]

Loyalty

Attempting to describe what it means to have a loyal friend, one of my students put it this way: "When everyone else is against you, they stick by you." Loyalty, then, is being true and faithful to a friend. This quality is perhaps best revealed and most appreciated in tough times.

During such times we find out how much our friends care about us. Loyalty is particularly important in marriage, where, in the name of fun, some newlyweds play a cruel game—making fun in public of their spouse's newly revealed idiosyncrasies or weaknesses—the bride's inability to cook, the groom's deficiencies as a handyman, or the like. The person being criticized may even smile, but such things inflict pain and feel like betrayal. After all, if there is anyone in the world we ought to be able to depend on for support, it is our spouse, and in marriage we need to be able to lift when our partner is discouraged, to love when loving is not easy, and to be there when others may deride the one we love. Learn to be loyal to your friends—it is marvelous preparation for marriage.

Self-Control

Self-control is defined as the restraint one is able to exercise over one's own impulses, emotions, or desires. Being able to exercise such control is a sign of maturity and is an attribute that is particularly valuable in a friend or a marriage partner. Elder Milton R. Hunter, a former General Authority, has said, "I believe the lack of self-control is one of the most common contributing factors of unhappiness and discord."[18] The lack of self-control in relationships is manifest in many ways. Here are some examples:

- Displaying anger or throwing temper tantrums
- Not doing what we say we will do
- Not controlling our physical desires

Addressing this topic, President Ezra Taft Benson said: "Restraint and self-control must be ruling principles in the marriage relationship."[19] So it is in dating relationships. Remembering a friend who exercised self-control is usually a pleasant experience. Some of the elements of self-control are patience, restraint, and unselfishness. Self-control gives us the ability to postpone present wants and desires. A good way to measure self-control is in fasting, which requires disciplining our natural desire for food and drink. If a person is able to fast, it demonstrates patience, restraint, and reliance upon our Father in Heaven.

Respect

Respect is a feeling of admiration, which generally has to be earned. When we respect someone, we hold that person in high regard. Having respect also means refraining from interfering with others' agency—we allow them to be themselves. When we respect someone, we also desire the very best for them. Many relationships end because one of the parties through his or her actions forfeits the right to be admired. I have heard young people say, "I couldn't stay in the relationship because I had lost respect for him or her."

What causes us to respect or lose respect for another person? If any of the smaller foundation blocks are not in place, respect dies. For example:

We earn respect when we are:	*We forfeit respect when we are:*
Honest	Dishonest
Dependable	Undependable
Communicative	Uncommunicative
Kind	Unkind
Loyal	Disloyal
Self-controlled	Undisciplined

Respect always motivates us to want to do and be the very best for the other person. It also motivates us to be kind and caring toward him or her. The quickest ways to lose respect in a relationship is to engage in immoral behavior or to be dishonest. How can we respect one who attempts to violate our chastity or who is untruthful with us? Contrary to the belief of some people that to "get along, you have to 'go along,'" the only way to gain the respect of those you date is to set a high standard of behavior and stick to it! I am appalled by reports I receive from Latter-day Saint young women who describe the poor conduct of some of our returned missionaries. There is absolutely no excuse for a returned missionary, one who has made sacred covenants in the temple, to trifle with the virtue of a young woman. How can a young woman have respect for such a person! By the same token, how can a young man respect a young woman who does not maintain high standards?

Elder Hugh W. Pinnock has given us this warning: "Men and women who do not have a wholesome respect for regulations during the dating process will often continue to break the rules after the word 'yes' at the altar is spoken."[20]

Trust

Trust is one of the highest achievements of a true friendship, and it too is a quality that must be earned. When we totally trust others we have absolute confidence in them. We believe they will do what they say they will do. We are willing to entrust to such a person our innermost wishes, fears, and concerns. Why? Because they have demonstrated to us that they will not violate our confidence in them. Trust and respect are mutual partners, for it is difficult to have one without the other. How can you trust someone who has not earned your respect?

Commitment

When we respect and trust another person, we are willing to commit ourselves to them in the highest regard. Speaking of his own commitment to his disciples, Jesus put it this way, "Greater love hath no man than this, that a man lay down his life for his friends" (John 15:13). To give your life for a friend would require a total commitment to that person. If we were to do so, it would be because we care about our beloved even more than we care about our own life. Imagine the relationship you would have to have with a person to lay down your life for them. Wouldn't that relationship have to be built on honesty, open communication, common interests and values, and mutual respect? Is it likely we would ever consider laying down our life for someone we didn't admire or respect or with whom we shared nothing in common?

When all these building blocks have been developed and are in place, the result is a lasting friendship, a friendship that can endure all the unforeseen problems and challenges of marriage.

I began this chapter on friendship with a quote from Elder Marion D. Hanks. I would like to end with another of his statements: "Married people should be *best friends;* no relationship on earth needs friendship as much as marriage. . . . Friendship in a marriage is so important. It blows away the chaff and takes the kernel, rejoices in the uniqueness of the other, listens patiently, gives generously, forgives freely. Friendship will motivate one to cross the room one day and say, 'I'm sorry. I didn't mean that.' It will not pretend perfection nor demand it. It will not insist that both respond exactly the same in every thought and feeling, but it will bring to the union honesty, integrity. There will be repentance and forgiveness in every marriage—every good marriage—and respect and trust."[21]

Assignment

Ask yourself, "What kind of a friend am I?" by answering the following questions:

1. Am I honest in my relationships?

2. Am I willing to take time to get to know someone rather than trying to push the relationship too fast?

3. Am I kind to others?

4. Can people depend on me?

5. Do I have or am I trying to develop a sense of humor?

6. Am I generally cheerful and pleasant to be around?

7. Am I loyal to my friends?

8. Am I learning to control my emotions and passions?

9. Can people trust me?

10. Do I merit the respect of those I date by keeping high moral standards?

CHAPTER 14

Christlike Love

"Charity is the pure love of Christ" (Moroni 7:47).

A marriage based on romantic love and friendship can probably endure the tests and trials of life. But for love between a married man and woman to last forever and to reach its full potential, it must include God, our Heavenly Father. When we invite the Lord into our marriage, we have a more complete love because his Spirit is there. This complete love can be diagrammed as follows:

Romantic love and friendship do not constitute a perfect love until we add to them the pure love of Christ. One of the meanings of the word *perfect* is "complete." How does the pure love of Christ make the love between a man and a woman more complete or more perfect? Such love is characterized by godly attributes. In the Book of Mormon, the prophet Mormon called these godly qualities "charity," or "the pure love of Christ," and described them this way: "And charity suffereth long, and is kind, and envieth not, and is not puffed up, seeketh not her own, is not easily provoked, thinketh no evil, and rejoiceth not in iniquity but rejoiceth in the truth, beareth all things, believeth all things, hopeth all things, endureth all things" (Moroni 7:45).

Mormon continues by saying, "If [we] have not charity, [we] are nothing." He then tells us to "cleave unto charity." The word *cleave* as it is used here means to hold tight to or to remain faithful to. He then gives us three reasons why this pure love of Christ, or charity, is so important (see Moroni 7:46–47):

1. "Charity never faileth"—it holds up under pressure.
2. It "endureth forever"—it lasts through this mortal life and into eternity.
3. "Whoso is found possessed of it at the last day, it shall be well with him."

A marriage in which a man and a woman each possess these attributes will endure the trials and tests that come to every marriage. The following chart helps you see more clearly why this is true. Let's review the qualities or the characteristics of this pure love as described by the Apostle Paul in 1 Corinthians 13—what it is and what it is not.

The Qualities of Christlike Love	What It Is	What It Is Not
Suffereth long	Patient	Anxious
Is kind	Kind	Hurtful
Envieth not	Supportive	Jealous
Vaunteth not	Modest	Proud/Boastful
Is not puffed up	Humble	Arrogant
Doth not behave unseemly	Polite	Rude
Seeketh not her own	Unselfish	Self-centered
Is not easily provoked	Nondefensive	Irritable/Short-tempered
Thinketh no evil	Trusting	Suspicious
Rejoiceth not in iniquity	Righteous	Evil-minded
Beareth all things	Submissive	Resistant
Believeth all things	Faithful	Doubtful
Hopeth all things	Optimistic	Pessimistic
Endureth all things	Durable	Temporary

Consider the contrasting qualities. Those on the right suggest *selfishness* while those on the left describe *selflessness*. Imagine the joy of having a friend who possessed these marvelous attributes. Imagine being married to such a person—one whose focus is serving and blessing the lives of others and who would willingly sacrifice his or her own comforts to ensure the happiness of his or her friend or partner. Think how the practice of these Christlike qualities enhances friendship and romance.

This is what is intended when we are told we ought to bring Christ into our marriage. He is our example, and when we are able to think and do as he would think and do, it will touch every aspect of our relationship with our companion—physical, social, intellectual, emotional, and spiritual.

Such love also gives us the ability to love others in spite of their faults and failings. This is precisely how Christ loves us. None of us will marry the "perfect person"; we will always find imperfections in others. The exercise of Christlike love gives us the ability to see beyond these shortcomings and envision the person as he or she may become. We are therefore more able to be patient, kind, and supportive of him or her. The Prophet Joseph Smith described the power of the pure love of Christ: "Nothing is so much calculated to lead people to forsake sin as to take them by the hand, and watch over them with tenderness. When persons manifest the least kindness and love to me, O what power it has over my mind, while the opposite course has a tendency to harrow up all the harsh feelings and depress the human mind."[1]

What a formula for success in human relationships!

President David O. McKay made reference to this kind of love when he said: "Service is a great part of love—the placing of others' needs before our own—service to one's Church, family, friends and all with whom one associates in daily living.

" 'If you love me, you will keep my commandments'—you will love your fellow men—and demonstrate that love by acts of kindness, consideration and thoughtfulness. Hate, envy and strife shall be crowded out as love for fellow men and for God fills every human heart."[2]

When we possess this Christlike dimension of perfect love, it will enable love to grow, even if the physical part of a relationship is taken away. President Spencer W. Kimball illustrated this by relating a personal experience: "For many years I saw a strong man carry his tiny, emaciated, arthritic wife to meetings and wherever she could go. There could be no sexual expression. Here was a selfless indication of affection. I think that is pure love."[3]

But how, you might ask, do I receive the pure love of Christ in my life? Elder Boyd K. Packer has answered this question: "Oh, youth, if you could know, the requirements of the Church are the highway to love, with guardrails securely in place, with guide signs plainly marked, with help along the way. How foolish is the youth who feels that the Church is a fence around love to keep him out. How unfortunate to resent counsel and restraints. How fortunate is the young person who follows the standards of the Church, even if just from sheer obedience or habit, for he will find a rapture and a joy fulfilled."[4]

The key is obedience. As you try to simply do what the Lord has asked you to do, you can grow in your ability to love as Jesus Christ has loved. Writing when he was serving as provost of Brigham Young University, Elder Bruce C. Hafen explained that these qualities of Christlike love are, however, not developed entirely through our own efforts. "Rather, charity is bestowed upon the true followers of Christ. (Moroni 7:48). Its source, like all other blessings of the Atonement, is the grace of God. Said Moroni, 'I prayed unto the Lord that he would give unto the Gentiles grace, that they might have charity' (Ether 12:36)."[5]

These qualities of godliness are a gift of God because of the Atonement of Jesus Christ. Through our Savior's love, sacrifice, and grace, we can be blessed to love as he loves. When God is a partner in our relationships, our focus is to become like him. We do this by following his Son, Jesus Christ. As we follow our Savior, we begin to acquire the qualities of godliness, the chief quality being the pure love of Christ. President Gordon B. Hinckley said, "I am one who believes that love, like faith, is a gift of God."[6] In a letter to his son, Moroni, Mormon explained that it is the Holy Ghost that fills us with this Christlike love: "And the first fruits of repentance is baptism; and baptism cometh by faith unto the fulfilling the commandments; and the fulfilling the commandments bringeth remission of sins;

"And the remission of sins bringeth meekness, and lowliness of heart; and because of meekness and lowliness of heart cometh the visitation of the Holy Ghost, *which Comforter filleth with hope and perfect love*, which love endureth by diligence unto prayer, until the end shall come, when all the saints shall dwell with God" (Moroni 8:25–26; emphasis added).

Through the influence of the Holy Ghost, we acquire the characteristics of the pure love of Christ. Elder Parley P. Pratt explained how this happens. Note carefully how the Holy Ghost refines and develops the physical, social, intellectual, emotional, and spiritual aspects of love: "[The Holy Ghost] quickens all the intellectual faculties, increases, enlarges, expands, and purifies all the natural passions and affections, and adapts them by the gift of wisdom to their lawful use. It inspires, develops, cultivates, and matures all the fine-toned sympathies, joys, tastes, kindred feelings, and affections of our nature. It inspires virtue, kindness, goodness, tenderness, gentleness, and charity. It develops beauty of person, form and features. It tends to health, vigor, animation, and social feeling. It develops and invigorates all the faculties of the physical and intellectual man. It strengthens, invigorates, and gives tone to the nerves. In short, it is, as it were, marrow to the bone, joy to the heart, light to the eyes, music to the ears, and life to the whole being."[7]

Does this help you understand why it is so important to live the gospel of Jesus Christ? Do you see the great blessings that can come to a marriage when the Lord is invited into that relationship?

You might wonder how the temple can assist you in acquiring Christlike love. The ordinances of the temple endow us with greater power to become like Jesus Christ. As we keep the covenants we make in the endowment and sealing ordinances, God expands our abilities to give and to receive love. When we kneel at the altar and enter into the new and everlasting covenant of marriage, the Lord is invited to be a partner in our marriage. We can then experience love unknown to those who have not made such covenants. Elder Bruce R. McConkie said, "I am firmly convinced that it is possible for a man or a woman to love his or her companion abundantly more in this thing which is called the new and everlasting covenant of marriage than it is ever possible to love such an individual outside this order of marriage, because we are entitled to have, and we do have, all of the normal and wholesome affection that does and should exist between the sexes and then in addition to that, we can have in our family the sanctifying influence of the love of Christ. We can have a love which is abiding and eternal and which never ceases and never ends but will grow and increase until the perfect day is attained."[8]

I know this to be true. You can share with the one you marry a love that is based on Jesus Christ. This love is a gift from God to you as you strive to keep the covenants you have made. This pure love will help you and your companion weather any storm, overcome any problem, and grow closer together and to your Father in Heaven. Elder Parley P. Pratt described how an understanding of eternal marriage, as revealed through the Prophet Joseph Smith, helped him to feel this eternal type of love: "It was Joseph Smith who taught me how to prize the endearing relationships of father and mother, husband, wife; of brother and sister, son and daughter.

"It was from him that I learned that the wife of my bosom might be secured to me for time and all eternity; and that the refined sympathies and affections which endeared us to each other emanated from the fountain of divine eternal love. . . . I had loved before, but I knew not why. But now I loved—with a pureness—an intensity of elevated exalted feeling."[9]

As we conclude this chapter, I must be very candid with you. This has been the most challenging chapter to put into writing. I have worried that some young people might skip this chapter, feeling that it was somehow not relevant in their lives. I have also been concerned that the ideas expressed herein might not be clear or easy to understand. After all, as I said in the introduction, to describe love, particularly Christlike love, is not easy. But I want so much for you to grasp how important it is to make the Lord the center of your life and your relationships. Perhaps, in conclusion, this illustration might help.

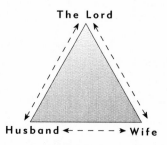

If we focus on the Lord in our marriage and seek earnestly to please him and to acquire his characteristics, think of the difference it would make, not only in our ability to love our spouse but in our spouse's capacity to love us. A husband and wife who take God into their partnership will receive the gift of Christlike love, which will introduce a sweetness and harmony they could not otherwise achieve. At the same time, by keeping their eye on the eternal potential of their relationship and striving to keep their temple covenants, they will tend to live beyond the moment with its mundane frustrations and challenges. That model is, I believe, what the Lord had in mind when he said, "Marriage is ordained of God unto man" (D&C 49:15).

Assignment

1. Carefully read Moroni 7:45–48 and note those things Moroni says we must do to receive the pure love of Christ.

2. List the ways the sacrament ordinance can assist you in receiving Christlike love.

3. Consider the following, which compares the enduring or lasting power of the three dimensions of love:

   ROMANTIC LOVE: Lasts a relatively short time; typically ends in divorce.

   ROMANTIC + FRIENDSHIP LOVE: Lasts until death.

   ROMANTIC + FRIENDSHIP + CHRISTLIKE LOVE: Lasts for eternity.

Section 3 Summary Points

1. There are three dimensions of love: romance, friendship, and Christlike love.

2. Romantic love was given to us by God and is important in furthering the plan of salvation.

3. To prepare yourself for a celestial marriage, you must keep the expression of romantic love within the bounds the Lord has set.

4. To build an enduring relationship, become friends before you become sweethearts.

5. Christlike love is a gift bestowed upon those who love and serve the Lord.

6. We must not be fooled by Satan's half-truths relative to romantic love.

Choosing

FOR ETERNITY

"The question 'Whom shall I marry?' is an important one to ask, for the proper answer to this question brings a proper answer to many others. If you marry the proper 'whom' and if you marry in the proper 'where,' then you will have an infinitely better chance of happiness throughout all eternity" (Spencer W. Kimball, "The Importance of Celestial Marriage," *Ensign*, October 1979, 3).

CHAPTER 15

The Secret to Successful Dating

*"Behold, will ye reject these words? Will ye reject
the words of the prophets?" (Jacob 6:8).*

A college professor planned an experiment to explore the psychol-
ogy of mate selection. In one of his classes were some football
players and some female cheerleaders. He took one of the football
players aside and made the following proposition: "You want a good
grade in this class, and I'm going to work you a deal whereby you can
get a B. All you have to do is pay some attention to Sally. She is the
brown-haired girl who sits three seats behind you. I want you to talk
with her after class and make an attempt to get to know her."

The football player replied, "But she's not very good-looking, and
I'm not really attracted to her."

The professor replied, "Maybe not, but that's the deal. Accept it or
earn a grade on your own."

Getting a good grade was important to the young man, and so he
accepted the assignment. The next day he made it a point to talk with
Sally. He began walking to class with her, called her occasionally on
the telephone, and sat next to her in class. Some of the cheerleaders
couldn't believe it. They wondered why a popular, good-looking football player would be interested in a girl like Sally.

After a few weeks the professor called the football player into his
office and said, "Well, it looks like you've earned a B. Now, how
would you like to earn an A?"

"I would," said the football player. "What do I need to do?"

The professor replied, "Take Sally on a date."

Thinking it was an easy way to get an A, the football player said, "Are you serious? That's all I have to do?"

"That's all."

"Okay, I'll do it."

He took Sally on one date, and then two, and you guessed it—he ended up marrying her. When the professor asked him what had happened, the young man explained, "After I got to know her, she became beautiful to me."

That the young man would come to feel this way is not so far-fetched. Perhaps you have had a similar experience in going to the movies. The first time the main character's face is projected on the screen—close up and huge—haven't you sometimes thought that he or she is not all that attractive? But given a chance to study the face and observe the personality through the course of the movie, you find that person becoming more appealing. After ninety minutes of exposure, you will often have formed an entirely different opinion of that person, finding them in many ways appealing and attractive.

This illustrates a powerful truth about relationships. Physical appearance is only one facet of an individual's makeup. But if that is the only criterion you use in evaluating someone, you are likely to miss out on meeting many interesting, fun, and unique people.

From my vantage point as a teacher, I have often stood in front of a new group of students and observed how many of the young people have already been written off by other members of the class. In many instances I have wanted to shake some of the young men and say to them, "Open your eyes! While you are using superficial things to measure the worth of these young women, you are overlooking the very qualities you would most value in a friend or a wife or the mother of your children." Many young women are equally short-sighted, summarily dismissing some of the young men because they don't measure up to some preconceived notion of what is "cool."

Some cultures have taken this aspect of mate selection right out of the picture. I traveled on an airplane on one occasion with a woman who had been born and raised in India. She was now a citizen of the

United States and was working for the State Department. She had also recently married and told me that hers had been an "arranged" marriage. That is, her parents had chosen the young man she had married.

I asked her if she had dated her husband before they were married. She said she hadn't.

"How, then, did you know you were in love?" I asked.

She told me that love before marriage had not been an issue. It was expected that she and her husband would learn to love each other after they were married.

I asked her what she thought of our custom of dating. Her reply was very interesting: "Your culture places most of the emphasis on the physical qualities. That is why I believe there is such a high divorce rate in the United States. Your dating system encourages people to focus on the wrong thing."

Focusing on physical looks is only one of the pitfalls of dating. There are many others. It is such a perilous and tension-filled activity that many young people give up on dating. But dating is a very important activity. It is the usual process through which most people find the person they will marry. Dating is also the arena in which you learn and practice the interpersonal skills that will help you be a good marriage partner. And to add to the significance of dating, consider that the choices you make in your dating years will affect the rest of your life. Let me put it this way: if you begin dating at sixteen and marry at twenty-three and you live for seventy-eight years, you will have taken just seven years to decide how happy or unhappy you will be for the next fifty-five years of your life . . . and on into eternity.

You, therefore, have some important decisions to make regarding dating. Who will you date? What types of activities will you do on dates? What if you do not date much or do not particularly want to date? The decisions you make will almost certainly determine whether or not you marry in the holy temple, and successful dating is dating that prepares you to one day be married for time and all eternity.

Whom will you listen to when it comes to setting dating standards? Friends? TV or movie personalities? Rock musicians? What will make those seven critical years the most productive and successful possible?

For thirty years I have been involved in the lives of young people like you. I have watched them date, become engaged, and have been privileged to attend many of their marriage ceremonies, both in and out of the temple. Based on what I have observed, here is the secret to successful dating: *Those young people who follow the dating guidelines given by the Lord and by Church leaders have the greatest chance of achieving happy, celestial marriages.*

Elder Henry B. Eyring of the Quorum of the Twelve emphasized this when he said: "Every time in my life when I have chosen to delay following inspired counsel or decided that I was an exception, I came to know that I had put myself in harm's way. Every time that I have listened to the counsel of prophets, felt it confirmed in prayer, and then followed it, I have found that I moved toward safety. Along the path, I have found that the way had been prepared for me and the rough places made smooth. God led me to safety along a path which was prepared with loving care, sometimes prepared long before."[1]

This I also know from personal experience.

May I recommend ten guidelines to you that will make dating a productive, safe, gospel-centered experience:

1. Avoid early steady dating.

Steady dating limits your exposure to new friends. It focuses your attention on one person when you should be getting to know many people. The purpose of dating is to help prepare you to choose an eternal companion. Many young adults have told me they wish they could go back and change their high school years. What would they change? Steady dating. It ought to also be evident that dating one person exclusively, over an extended period of time, invites a familiarity that can also lead to sexual immorality.

2. Date a little, date a lot, but stick to your standards.

I have known a number of young women who had very few dates either in high school or later. Others date a lot. I have known young men who were so shy they dated very little. Many of these same young people, as they matured, began to date more. Dating can be a healthy way to develop skills essential to marriage, such as how to communicate with members of the opposite sex and how to give and receive love and affection. It is important, however much you date, that you stick to gospel standards.

I have known some young women who decided that to get a date they needed to lower their standards. I have also known many young women who hardly dated at all but held to their standards and eventually married in the temple. Let me tell you about one such girl.

I first met Janice when she applied for a job as our institute of religion secretary. She was an impressive young single adult, extremely mature and competent for her age. After she was hired and I got to know her, she told me that during high school she had only had one date and that was to the senior prom. Janice said that while other girls lowered their standards just to get dates, she was determined that she wanted to be worthy of the right kind of guy. Because of her commitment, she radiated a wholesomeness and goodness that could be felt by those who knew her.

A young man returned from his mission and began attending classes at our institute. One day he came in to see me. He said, "I am really attracted to your secretary. She seems to radiate something special. I wonder if you would mind if I asked her on a date."

"First of all," I said, "she is a very special girl and you don't need my permission to ask her out. But I think you've made a great choice!"

A few days later Janice came beaming into the institute. She said, "You will never guess what happened." I didn't have the heart to tell her what I knew.

"Last night I got a call from David, and he asked me out on a date. It will be the second date of my life."

Well, they dated for a year and were then married in the temple. I'll never forget standing in the sealing room with Janice and David. Radiant and happy on her special day, she said to me, "This was sure worth waiting for!"

3. Be honest yet sensitive in dating relationships.

In our society, dating can be a very challenging experience. For some young men it is a terrifying thing to ask a girl for a date because of the fear of rejection. For this reason, girls need to be sensitive to boys when turning down a date. Such responses as "I'm busy that night" or "I have to baby-sit" do not communicate what the girl may really be thinking. If you say instead, "I'm busy Saturday, but I'm free next weekend," it lets him know you have an interest and aren't just brushing him off. What does a young woman say if she has no interest in dating the young man? I have found the best way to deal with this is not to play games. It is kinder to be honest and simply say, "You're a nice guy, but to be honest, I'm not interested in dating you."

4. Place yourself in situations where you can meet the type of person you want to marry.

Young people who desire to date but do not date a lot should consider making themselves more available by being in places where they can meet active Latter-day Saints. Attending firesides, taking institute classes, going to YSA conferences, dances, and other uplifting activities can provide opportunities for association and dating.

I have known a number of capable, wonderful Latter-day Saint young women who found they had little opportunity to date and who had the courage to change the location of where they were living or working and who as a result met the person they eventually married.

5. Be selective of those you agree to date.

Though it occasionally happens in some other way, you will likely marry some person you have dated. You need, therefore, to ask yourself the question, Is this person likely to be someone I could marry? Elder Bruce C. Hafen emphasized this when he said: "In your searching for the fulfillment of your romantic longings, always live for the presence of the Holy Spirit, that you may have it as your constant guide. Don't date someone you already know you would not ever want to marry. If you fall in love with someone you should not marry, you can't expect the Lord to guide you away from that person after you are already emotionally commited."[2]

6. Plan the types of dates that will help you get to know each other.

One of the major purposes of dating is to get to know other people. As you do this you will also get to know yourself. Through dating you will also learn to identify the qualities and characteristics you desire in an eternal companion. Therefore, be creative. Don't limit yourself to going to movies, dances, or parties. Picnics, bike rides, bowling or other sports, study dates, or service projects and the like provide good opportunities to become acquainted and explore each other's personalities.

7. Be selective of the places you go and what you do on dates.

There are so many places you can go today that are not worthy of the Spirit of the Lord. Some movies, dance halls, and concerts obviously do not promote gospel standards. You certainly wouldn't expect to find an eternal companion in a bar, which some young people frequent on the rationalization that they serve good food or book top musical groups. Moroni has given us a very simple test: "For behold, the Spirit of Christ is given to every man, that he may know good from evil; wherefore, I show unto you the way to judge; for every thing which inviteth to do good, and to persuade to believe in Christ, is sent forth by the power and gift of Christ; wherefore ye may know with a perfect knowledge it is of God" (Moroni 7:16).

Do not place yourself in situations where you are likely to be tempted. I often ask young people who are having challenges staying virtuous, "What kinds of activities lead to the temptation to be immoral?" The answers are usually the same: "It happens when we are laying on the couch cuddling." "We have trouble when we are in the bedroom studying together." *Avoid places that invite temptation and activities that lead to sexual intimacy!* Remember, if you choose to go to places that promote evil or to places that invite temptation, you go by yourself! The Spirit of the Lord will not be there.

8. Plan to conclude your dates at a reasonable hour.

After the movie is over, the restaurant is closed, or the dance has let out are the times when young people usually get into difficulty. It takes energy to resist temptation, and when we are tired, we are more vulnerable. A wise young man or young woman will establish a curfew for themselves and abide by it. Staying out past a reasonable hour is simply inviting temptation.

9. Be modest in your dress.

We have been counseled by our Church leaders to dress modestly. Why? Because the way we dress influences the way we behave and also sends a message to other people. For example, when we attend church we wear "church dress." This generally puts us on our best behavior and communicates to others that we love and respect the Lord. When you dress for a date, make sure you do not send the wrong signal. This counsel applies equally to both young men and young women.

10. Take responsibility for your behavior while dating.

Dating carries with it a great responsibility. You must be mature enough to govern yourself without parental supervision. Young men have a responsibility to ensure the physical safety and to preserve the virtue of the young women they date. Young women have a responsibility to encourage young men to keep the commandments and to honor the priesthood they bear.

The dating years can be a great time to have fun, get to know yourself, and identify the qualities you want in your future husband or wife. Following the teachings of Church leaders will bless your life. These teachings will free you from the two greatest contributors to unhappiness: *remorse* and *regret*.

Assignment

Consider carefully this question: "What standards have you set or will you set to guide your dating experiences?"

CHAPTER 16

What You Need to Know Should You Choose to Date Nonmembers

"Be ye not unequally yoked together with unbelievers" (2 Corinthians 6:14).

When I ask my students "What is the single most important factor that will determine whom you will marry?" they respond in many different ways. But they all seem to agree that we inevitably choose our spouse from among those we date and hang around with. Consider the influence your friends have on you. We usually become like our friends—sharing common beliefs, interests, and activities. True friends respect our standards and help us live them. Others we know may seem to be jealous of what we stand for and seek to tear us down. Those are the kinds of friends we need to careful of.

When asked whether Church members ought to date nonmembers, many young Latter-day Saints respond by saying, "It doesn't matter whom you date if that person has similar standards to yours." I've heard others say, "Why not? Some members have lower standards than nonmembers!" Still others might argue, "Isn't it better to marry a nonmember than to never marry at all?" This is a difficult topic, particularly if you live in an area where there are few Latter-day Saints to date.

You have been given your agency in this matter. The Lord will not choose your husband or wife for you. With agency, particularly as it relates to choosing a companion, you have a serious responsibility! It might help to remember that the person you choose to marry will influence not only your entire mortal life but the course of your eternal life. Here are some guidelines for you to think about as you decide whether you will date nonmembers.

1.Church leaders have counseled you not to date nonmembers or members who are not faithful.

One who has advised you "not [to] take the chance of dating nonmembers, or members who are untrained or faithless" is President Spencer W. Kimball.[1] Another is President Gordon B. Hinckley, who has said, "Your chances for a happy and lasting marriage will be far greater if you will date those who are active and faithful in the Church. Such dating is most likely to lead to marriage in the temple."[2] On another occasion President Hinckley said, "You young men, fall in love with Latter-day Saint girls. And you young women, fall in love with Latter-day Saint boys. You will be happier if you do so. You will be happier because you will understand one another and appreciate one another's values, and you will be grateful all of your days if you will do that."[3]

Do you believe this counsel, or do you think it applies to someone else?

2. You marry those you date and hang around with.

I've heard some young people say: "I date nonmembers just to have fun. I'm not going to marry outside the temple." Elder Mark E. Peterson, a former member of the Quorum of the Twelve Apostles, counseled young people: "What kind of a crowd are you going with? What kind of a person will you marry? You will marry from the crowd you go with; and if you choose the nonchurchgoing crowd, remember that is what you will get, and all it includes. Think, consider it carefully, and then act safely."[4]

President Spencer W. Kimball put it this way: "Choosing a marriage partner is a vital decision. The greatest single factor affecting what you are going to be tomorrow, your activity, your attitudes, your eventual destiny . . . is the one decision you make that moonlit night when you ask that individual to be your companion for life. That's the most important decision of your entire life! It isn't where you are going to school, or what lessons you are going to study, or what your major is, or how you are going to make your living. These, though important, are incidental and nothing compared with the important decision that you make when you ask someone to be your companion for eternity."[5]

President Kimball also said, "You cannot afford to take a chance on falling in love with someone who may never accept the gospel."[6] What chance are you taking should you fall in love with someone who cannot go to the temple? You are putting at jeopardy not only your happiness here on earth, but your eternal destiny! And this is to say nothing of the turmoil you will likely introduce into the lives of your children as they come along and decisions have to be made about their own religious instruction.

3. Most people not of our faith do not join the Church after marriage.

You probably know someone who joined the Church after marrying a member. What you might not know is that a majority do not join the Church. President Spencer W. Kimball has written: "Yes, a small minority are finally baptized [after marrying Church members]. Some good men and women have joined the Church after the interfaith marriage and have remained most devout and active. God bless them! We are proud of them and grateful for them. These are our blessed minority.

"Others who do not join the Church are still kind, considerate, and cooperative, and permit the member spouse to worship and serve according to the Church pattern. . . . The majority, however, do not join the Church. Surveys have indicated that only one of seven finally join the Church—the odds are against the others. And nearly half of those [members] who marry out of the Church become inactive."[7]

Risky business, wouldn't you say? I have a young friend who took such a chance. She told me, "The Lord didn't tell me to marry him, but I was willing to take the risk. I was willing to do so because I felt deep in my heart he would one day join the Church and take me to the temple. But he hasn't yet."

There are two questions you need to carefully consider:

Do you want a Latter-day Saint home where you can enjoy all the blessings of living the gospel? Where do you want to spend eternity?

The fact is you can voluntarily lock the door to your exaltation by the decisions you make as to whom you will date, fall in love with, and marry. President Brigham Young felt so strongly about this that he said: "There is not a young man in our community who would not be willing to travel from here to England to be married right, if he understood things as they are; there is not a young woman in our community, who loves the gospel and wishes its blessings, that would be married in any other way; they would live unmarried until they could be married as they should be, if they lived until they were as old as Sarah before she had Isaac born to her. Many of our brethren have married off their children without taking this into consideration, and thinking it a matter of little of importance. I wish we all understood this in the light in which heaven understands it."[8]

4. You might place yourself in compromising situations should you date nonmembers.

People not of our faith usually don't share our values, beliefs, and standards. Some see nothing wrong with going to a bar or to a party where alcohol and drugs are being used. Imagine the dilemma an LDS young woman could get herself into if she were strongly attracted to a nonmember boy who does not believe in the Word of Wisdom. Picture the temptation experienced by an LDS young man who is dating a nonmember young woman who does not understand the importance of chastity. In the name of being tolerant or acting out of a desire to associate with a certain person, some Latter-day Saint youth are willing to date nonmembers, feeling they can watch but not participate. Peer pressure being what it is, that is a dangerous practice. Remember the verse from Alexander Pope:

> Vice is a monster of so frightful a mien [face],
> As to be hated needs but to be seen;
> Yet seen too oft, familiar with her face,
> We first endure, then pity, then embrace.[9]

5. Should you choose to date and eventually marry a nonmember, you need to know it likely will not be easy.

Writing to members of the Church, the Apostle Paul counseled them: "Be ye not unequally yoked together with unbelievers" (2 Corinthians 6:14).

What did he mean by "unequally yoked"? A yoke is a wooden bar or frame that links two oxen. It serves to balance the load between them so that each pulls an equal share. What Paul was saying, then, was that when members of the Church (believers) are yoked (married) to nonmembers (unbelievers), it makes for an inefficient team, in a spiritual sense. Without shared values, beliefs, or feelings about the Lord, a couple is destined to struggle, and unless one acquiesces entirely to the other, there are bound to be major differences leading to conflict.

Commenting on Paul's statement, President Kimball said: "Without common faith, trouble lies ahead. When two people marry who have different standards, different approaches, and different backgrounds, it is a very difficult thing. There are exceptions, but the rule is a harsh and unhappy one. Religious differences imply wider areas of conflict. Church loyalties clash, and family loyalties clash. . . . Religious differences are fundamental differences."[10]

6. The best time to introduce the gospel is before you begin dating or before you are in a serious relationship.

I have known a number of LDS young women who have dated nonmembers, hoping their boyfriends would eventually join the Church so they could be married to them in the temple. It has been sad to see some of these girls invest two or three years in such an effort, only to be devastated emotionally when the relationship came to an end. Some of these nonmembers have told me that once a serious relationship was established, it made the whole religion thing all the harder to sort out. The fact that they were romantically involved placed a lot of pressure on them to join the Church for the wrong reasons. Therefore, the sooner you introduce your boyfriend or girlfriend to the gospel, the better off you both will be. *Your example of faithfulness will be the most important factor in your friend's decision whether to investigate the Church.*

An experience I had while teaching at the institute of religion at the University of Utah illustrates this. One day I received a telephone call from a young man who asked if he could visit with me. When he came to my office, he told me that he was a graduate student at the university and that one of the secretaries in his department was a member of the Church. He was attracted to her and had asked her on a date. Her response had been, "I am a member of The Church of Jesus Christ of Latter-day Saints, and I do not date anyone not of my faith."

The young man indicated to me that at first he had been very upset, but as time went on, he had begun to have a great deal of respect for her. He'd never met anyone who was so honest and up front with her convictions. He admired that in her and asked me if I could help him learn more about the gospel. I invited him to listen to the missionary discussions, which were taught in my office, and two months later, he was baptized.

The young woman who had set such a positive example for him then accepted an invitation to go on a date with him. A year later they were married in the Salt Lake Temple.

All stories will not, of course, turn out as happily as this one. But did you notice that the young man gained respect for the young woman because she stood up for her values and introduced the gospel to him *before* they began dating?

7. Should you marry outside the temple, you will deprive yourself of the blessings of Abraham.

God made significant promises to Abraham and his descendants. These promises include the privilege of holding the priesthood, administering the saving ordinances, and the blessing of being together as a family for all eternity. Abraham received these promises as a consequence of his righteousness when he married Sarah for time and all eternity. You will be promised these same blessings, on condition of *your* righteousness, when you are sealed to *your* spouse in the holy temple. That is the only way you can receive the blessings of

Abraham, and the temple is the only place on earth designated by God for you to receive these promises. One person alone cannot kneel at the altar; it takes two—two Latter-day Saints who are "equally yoked together," united in their faith, and worthy to be in the temple of God.

President Spencer W. Kimball emphasized this truth when he said: "No one who rejects the covenant of celestial marriage can reach exaltation in the eternal kingdom of God. . . .

"No one! It matters not how righteous they may have been, how intelligent or how well trained they are. No one will enter this highest glory unless he enters into the covenant, and this means the new and everlasting covenant of marriage."[11]

You will likely marry someone from among those you hang around with and date. The decisions you are making now will not only affect you, but also your children and untold numbers of your descendants in generations yet to come. Eternity is a long, long time. Please, choose wisely.

Assignment

1. Review the account of Abraham sending his servant to choose a wife for Isaac from among his believing kinfolk (see Genesis 24:1–4). Why was Abraham so concerned about whom Isaac married?

2. Read Genesis 27:46; 28:1–5. Why were Isaac and Rebecca so concerned about whom Jacob might marry?

3. Read Genesis 26:34–35. Why did Isaac and Rebecca experience such great sorrow over Esau? Why is your Heavenly Father so concerned about whom you marry? Consider this statement by Elder Richard G. Scott: "Choose good friends, those who have made similar decisions in their lives, those like yourself who are wise enough to live a life of order and restraint. When one gets off track, it is generally because the other kind of friends were chosen. Be surrounded by true friends who accept you the way you are and leave you better because of their association."[12]

4. Consider the disadvantages of marrying a less-active member of the Church or a nonmember.

CHAPTER 17

Ten Dimensions of an Eternal Relationship

*"And . . . they were of one heart
and one mind"(Moses 7:18).*

I f a couple is to be happily married, they need to assess several key areas in their relationship. To assist you in doing this, I am suggesting ten important considerations. If you are compatible and see eye-to-eye in these things, you will likely have a happy, satisfying, and eternal marriage.

1. Religion
2. Integrity/Honesty
3. Communication
4. Role preferences
5. Family/Friends
6. Resolving conflicts
7. Financial management
8. Physical intimacy/Children
9. Personality/Interests
10. Goals

Discussing these ten areas with the one you feel you are in love with will assist you in at least three ways:

First, the list will open communication on topics which are key to your relationship and which may need your attention.

Second, the list can help you identify potential problem areas in your relationship. You can then discuss these issues and work on solutions prior to getting married. Remember, changes are much easier to make before marriage.

Third, an awareness of potential problems will help you make the decision to get married with your mind as well as your heart. When we are in love or infatuated, our heart can overrule our better judgment. It's like a young woman once said to her parents, "Don't try to convince me not to marry him, I've already made up my mind." She might just as well have said, "I've already made up my *heart!*" If she had been in her right *mind*, she probably would not have married him, for her marriage ended in disaster. She later said, "I got married solely on emotion. I should have taken more time to evaluate what I was getting myself into."

1. Religion

You must decide together what part the gospel and Church activity will play in your life and home. Should you desire an eternal relationship, one based on the gospel of Jesus Christ, it will not be enough to just marry a member of the Church. You will want to marry someone who loves the Lord and who is as committed as you to an eternal framework. I asked a friend, whom I respect very much because of the challenges she has faced in her life, what she would say is the most important aspect of a good marriage. Without hesitation she said, "Spirituality. When the Lord is in your marriage and in your home, you can overcome almost any challenge."

Questions on Religion

- How important was the gospel in each of our families?
- How was the importance of the gospel shown in our families?
- Who took the lead in spiritual matters in our families?
- What priority does the Lord have in each of our lives right now?
- What will we do to keep the Lord a major priority in our home?
- How important will the following activities be in our home: family prayers, mealtime prayers, scripture study, family home evening, and Church and temple attendance?

- What will be our attitude toward Church callings?
- What will we do to maintain our individual testimonies?
- How important will it be in our home to pay our tithing?
- How will we ensure that we keep the Sabbath day holy?

2. Integrity/Honesty

One of the most important qualities in a marriage relationship is that of trust. Trust is built on integrity and honesty. Integrity is the measure of our ability to make and keep commitments. It is absolutely essential to a happy, enduring marriage. When problems and challenges arise—and they will—integrity is what keeps us true to our covenants with each other and with the Lord.

Honesty is the quality of being truthful with each other. When couples are honest with each other there are fewer surprises after marriage.

Questions on Integrity/Honesty

- In our relationship, have we followed through with commitments we have made to each other, or has there been a pattern of irresponsibility?
- What are the specific ways we have demonstrated integrity and honesty in our dealings with each other?
- What about Church callings? Have we each followed through and been responsible?
- What about with our employers? Have we been responsible and honest?
- Do we absolutely trust each other? If so, why? If not, why?
- Are either of us prone to make excuses for not following through or not keeping our commitments?

3. Communication

Newly married couples often say, "We just don't seem to communicate anymore!" The ability to share thoughts and feelings is critical to a successful marriage. If we have communicated poorly before marriage, it will be the same after—unless a couple does something about it.

To make a good marriage great, we must learn to share our feelings honestly and to listen to each other with both head and heart.

Questions on Communication

- Is our communication based on mutual respect and kindness?
- Have we been open and honest with each other? Or do we hide our feelings, expecting the other to discover what we are thinking?
- Do we each feel that the other person cares about our opinions and feelings?
- What do we do that shows we respect each other's opinions and feelings?
- Do either of us need to "be right" all the time? What problems has this created for us?
- Do we feel that we each listen while the other person is talking?
- Do we make time to share feelings? If not, why not?
- What specific things will we do after we are married to ensure that, with our busy lives, we make time for each other?
- What were the patterns of communication like in our families? Did each set of parents have open communication? What will we change or do similarly?

4. Role Preferences

Each partner brings to a marriage relationship ideas and expectations as to how a spouse should act. Many of these opinions are formed as we watch our parents interact with each other; others may be the result of the influence of the media, books, and movies. Elder James E. Faust has warned that we cannot trust the many conflicting voices that clamor about what women should or should not do in today's society.[1] The same is true with regard to the roles of men. You must be very careful to base your expectations on gospel principles, not the ideas of the world. Someone has suggested that we should have "preferences" rather than "expectations." An expectation is the way we "expect" another to behave. It can communicate an element of control over another person. A "preference" is what we would like the person to be. A couple should discuss before marriage what their preferences are. When we base our preferences on the gospel of Jesus Christ, we are on a solid foundation.

Questions on Role Preferences: Who Did the Following in Our Parents' Families?

Activity	Father	Mother	Both
Earn the living			
Prepare meals			
Clean the house			
Take care of the yard			
Take care of the car(s)			
Initiate family prayer and family home evening			
Change the baby's diapers			
Read to and put the children to bed			

- Who will do each of these in our marriage?
- What is his perception of an ideal wife?
- What is her perception of an ideal husband?

5. Family/Friends

One of the things that many single people often do not think about is the influence and impact their respective families will have on their marriage. The simple fact is that when we marry, we marry the entire family. Sometimes parents have a difficult time letting go of their children. Also, some children find it difficult to let go of parents. The scriptures teach clearly, "Therefore shall a man leave his father and his mother, and shall cleave unto his wife: and they shall be one flesh" (Genesis 2:24). Friends will also have an influence on a marriage and can either be a source of great support or a great distraction. Friends tend to be a reflection of ourselves. If you dislike his or her friends, you may actually be rejecting significant characteristics of your potential spouse.

Questions on Family

- What do we like about each other's family?
- If there are problems with in-laws, how might this impact our marriage?
- How much interaction should we have after marriage with our in-laws?
- Do our parents support our marriage?
- What traditions are important in each of our families?
- What traditions will we have?

Questions on Friends

- Do we like and get along with the same people?
- Do we have friends that either of us do not like? If so, how will we deal with this?
- When will we invite friends to our home, and how will we decide this?
- How will we treat each other in front of our friends?

6. Resolving Conflicts

Disagreements and conflicts are the source of many problems in a marriage. Because you come from different backgrounds, each with a unique personality and diverse experiences, it is certain that disagreements will occur. The way you deal with disagreements and with hurt feelings will affect how happy your marriage is. Some young people have the mistaken idea that the act of getting married will somehow change the patterns of conflict in the relationship. Most studies show that, if anything, being married intensifies any conflict in a relationship. So if you argue and fight a lot before you are married, do not expect that to decrease after marriage.

Perhaps the most damaging behavior to a relationship is anger. While angry, we are likely to say and do things that leave deep wounds and may, if not resolved, lead to unhappiness or divorce. Before getting married, couples should learn how to resolve disagreements in a sensitive, nonaggressive manner. It is possible to disagree and not be disagreeable. Elder Hugh W. Pinnock has given the following suggestions as to how to deal with disagreements:

"Do not feel that an intense disagreement in a marriage indicates that it cannot succeed. If we are to really communicate, we must be honest when we disagree. We must express hurts and let our feelings show. We can do this without becoming angry or inconsiderate. People who keep things bottled up inside are candidates for a variety of illnesses. And equally serious, that approach does not solve problems.

"Serious disagreements between marriage partners do not mean that the two are becoming allergic to one another or that the situation is hopeless. It merely means that they are human and they are not perfect. If they acknowledge their differences in a mature way, they will recognize that their marriage is okay. They simply have, in this situation, failed to communicate. They can work out their differences without jeopardizing their relationship."[2]

Couples who are happily married still have things they disagree about and things they wish their partner would change. But they have learned to accept many such differences and to live with them. The reason? They are best friends.

Questions on Resolving Conflicts

- How did each of our parents resolve conflicts?
- When we have disagreements, how do we resolve them?
- Do we argue a lot? If so, why? What can we do differently to resolve our differences? Have we learned to work out challenges together? If not, will being married likely change this pattern?
- Are we able to control anger? If not, what can we do before marriage to resolve this? Do we need to counsel with someone?
- Have we learned to say, "I'm sorry" when we hurt each other's feelings?

7. Financial Management

It may surprise you to learn that disagreement over money management is one of the major sources of marital discord. One study estimates that 89 percent of all divorces can be traced to quarrels and accusations over money.[3] Commenting on this statistic, Elder Marvin J.

Ashton said: "How important are money management and finances in marriage and family affairs? May I respond, 'Tremendously.'"[4]

Questions on Financial Management

- How will tithing fit into the management of our finances?
- What was the attitude of our parents toward debt? Toward saving? Budgeting?
- Who managed the money in each of our homes?
- How did our parents communicate about money matters?
- What will we do to ensure we do not go into debt?
- Do we agree about budgeting, saving, and investing?
- How will we handle credit cards?
- What types of bank accounts will we have?
- How will we see that bills are paid in a timely manner?
- Who will balance the checkbook?
- What types of purchases will we be able to be make individually? Which will we need to agree on?
- How responsible have each of us been in the past with regard to money management?
- How do we plan to support our family financially?

8. Physical Intimacy/Children

Elder Hugh B. Brown has given us this wise counsel: "Sex is not an unmentionable human misfortune, and certainly it should not be regarded as a sordid but necessary part of marriage. There is no excuse for approaching this most intimate relationship in life without true knowledge of its meaning and its high purpose. This is an urge which more insistently than others calls for self-control and intelligence."[5]

This dimension of marriage should be discussed only by couples who are in a serious relationship and contemplating marriage.

Questions on Physical Intimacy

- How was this area approached in each of our homes?
- Do we each feel comfortable talking about physical intimacy? If not, why not?
- What is our idea of romance?

- What will we do to keep romance alive after we are married?
- Do we respect each other's feelings about this matter?

One of the primary purposes of marriage is to bring children into the world. Many newlyweds have reported that they didn't have any major conflicts until they began having children. Bringing a baby into a home introduces a new dimension in the relationship. Talking about this area of marriage can help you prepare for your children.

Questions on Children

- When will we have children?
- How did our parents discipline us?
- How will we discipline our children?
- What will we do to raise our children in the gospel?
- What will we do once children are born to ensure that we continue to grow and to communicate with each other?

9. Personality/Interests

Too many people believe that, after marriage, they can mold or shape their intended spouse to conform to their liking. However, it is unrealistic to believe that can be done. Effecting any change in an individual is difficult, and, as pointed out in chapter 3, such an effort is usually successful only when it is self-motivated—not when it is forced by someone else. If you really don't like the way your potential spouse behaves, perhaps you should reconsider the relationship. Complaints that are most frequently made are in the areas of neatness, punctuality, orderliness, and personal hygiene. Another point of potential conflict is the difference in energy levels. If one person is very vigorous and the other is slower and more laid back, it could present some challenges. Again, one of the most important qualities you can possess is flexibility—the ability to deal with a situation without falling apart and to adapt to any differences. Much of the delight in marriage comes from sharing experiences. Obviously then, mutual interests are important if the marriage partners are to derive maximum enjoyment from their union.

Questions on Personality/Interests

- What do we enjoy about each other's personality?
- Do we have certain habits or behaviors we would like to see changed?
- Do we share common interests?
- Do we have conflicting interests that we need to resolve?
- Do we enjoy similar levels of energy?
- What compromises do we need to make?
- How do we each like to spend our time? Alone? With groups? With each other? How might these preferences impact our marriage?

10. Goals

As a married couple you will need to be pulling together and be headed in the same direction. It is therefore helpful to have a set of common goals or purposes. On this topic President Ezra Taft Benson has said: "Clearly understood goals bring our lives into focus just as a magnifying glass focuses a beam of light into one burning point. Without goals our efforts may be scattered and unproductive."[6]

Questions on Goals

- What do we want to accomplish in each of the following areas in the next two months? One year? Five years?

	Next 2 months	1 year	5 years
Spirituality			
Education			
Job/Career			
Housing			
Children			

- Are our goals compatible with the counsel of Church leaders?

The most stable marriages are those involving two people who have many things in common. You might want to think of it this way: similarities are like money in the bank; differences are like debts. "Liquidating" each difference will require patience, negotiation, and adaptation.

Assignment

Prioritize the ten areas below. Which do you feel is the most important in a relationship? Second, third, and so on? Does the one you love feel the same?

_____ Religion

_____ Integrity/Honesty

_____ Communication

_____ Family/Friends

_____ Resolving conflicts

_____ Financial management

_____ Physical intimacy/Children

_____ Role preferences

_____ Personality/Interests

_____ Goals

Researchers at BYU have created a test couples can take to assess the strength of their relationship. RELATE explores the markers in a premarital relationship that most accurately predict later compatibility in marriage. This test is relatively inexpensive and can be ordered by calling the Marriage Study Consortium at BYU, 801–378–4359.

CHAPTER 18

Dealing with Differences

*"And now I would that ye should be humble, and
be submissive and gentle; easy to be entreated; full
of patience and long-suffering" (Alma 7:23).*

If you have discussed the questions in the previous chapter with
the one you love, you have probably found that you are different in
many respects. If you are not in a relationship at this time, the questions might help you understand why previous relationships have not
developed into serious ones.

No matter how well we think we know each other before marriage,
we will still discover after we are married things we didn't know about
each other. President George Albert Smith is quoted as saying, "You
know, when I was growing up I never saw a difference of opinion
between my father and my mother. I used to think it was a miracle, and
after I had been married for twenty years, I knew it was a miracle."[1]

Always the realist, President Spencer W. Kimball observed: "Two
people coming from different backgrounds soon learn after the ceremony is performed that stark reality must be faced. There is no longer a
life of fantasy or of make-believe; we must come out of the clouds and
put our feet firmly on the earth. Responsibility must be assumed and
new duties must be accepted. Some personal freedoms must be relin-
quished, and many adjustments, unselfish adjustments, must be made.

"One comes to realize very soon after the marriage that the spouse
has weaknesses not previously revealed or discovered. The virtues

which were constantly magnified during courtship now grow relatively smaller, and the weaknesses which seemed so small and insignificant during courtship now grow to sizable proportions. The hour has come for understanding hearts, for self-appraisal, and for good common sense, reasoning and planning. The habits of years now show themselves; the spouse may be stingy or prodigal, lazy or industrious, devout or irreligious, may be kind and cooperative or petulant and cross, demanding or giving, egotistical or self-effacing. The in-law problem comes closer into focus, and the relationships of the spouses to them is again magnified."[2]

President Kimball wisely emphasized a number of points in this statement. It would be well for you to reread it very carefully. One point to think about is that people have a tendency to minimize weaknesses and magnify virtues before marriage. After marriage, weaknesses are magnified and virtues minimized. This idea can be illustrated as follows:

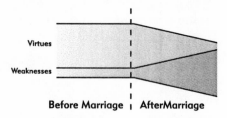

What kinds of problems might this create after marriage? To help minimize these problems, let's look at where differences come from and why we are the way we are. Then we can explore ways to resolve as many differences as we can before marriage. There are at least eight factors that have influenced us and shaped our personality.

1. Our Premortal Experiences

Each of us brings to mortality the attributes, talents, and gifts we acquired in premortality. Elder Bruce R. McConkie said that in our prior life we had friends and associates. "We were schooled and trained and taught in the most perfect educational system ever devised, and that by obedience to his eternal laws we developed infinite varieties and degrees of talents."[3]

It has been very evident with the birth of our five children that each came with his or her distinct personality. One of the ways to better understand ourselves is to receive a patriarchal blessing. This blessing can often provide insights into who we were before our mortal birth, who we are now with regard to our gifts and our talents, and who we may become. All patriarchal blessings provide two important bits of information: our lineage, and the promises given to Abraham to which we are entitled because of that lineage. A patriarchal blessing may also contain counsel, warnings, a description of gifts and talents, and promised blessings. To better understand your blessing, you might write several headings on a piece of paper; then organize the content of your blessing under them, as noted below:

- Lineage—the lineage through which your blessings and responsibilities are derived.
- Abrahamic promises—the promises given to Abraham, which you share, regarding resurrection and priesthood and temple blessings, including eternal marriage.
- Counsel—specific things the Lord counsels you to do.
- Warnings and admonitions—a blessing may specifically warn you of dangers, temptations, or pitfalls you may encounter in life or may declare certain things you are to pursue or accomplish.
- Gifts/Talents—The Lord may indicate to you the specific gifts you have brought with you into mortality and indicate how you are to use them.

Such an analysis may help you better understand your potential and be helpful also in preparing you more thoroughly for marriage. Though you may be tempted to share the content of your blessing with the one you love, its contents are sacred and highly personal. It is inappropriate to share it with others, although after you are married, you might choose to do so with your spouse.

2. Our Family in Mortality

The influence our earthly family has on us cannot be overemphasized. It is probably impossible to identify all the ways we have been shaped by our parents, siblings, and home life. These influences have determined the language we speak and helped sculpt our outlook on life, the way we relate to people, our attitudes and expectations, and our preferences, habits, and self-esteem.

Speaking of the influence of families on their children, the Lord has said: "Every spirit of man was innocent in the beginning; and God having redeemed man from the fall, men became again, in their infant state, innocent before God.

"And that wicked one cometh and taketh away light and truth, through disobedience, from the children of men, and because of the tradition of their fathers" (D&C 93:38–39).

The "tradition of their fathers" might refer to either the positive or negative influence had by our parents. Such things are often passed from one generation to the next. That is why many marriage counselors advise young people to look carefully at the family of the one they marry as well as at their own. Boys will carry on many of the characteristics of their father and girls of their mother. My wife brought that forcefully to my attention one day when she said, "I'm certainly glad I liked your father." When I asked, "Why do you say that?" she answered, "Because the longer I live with you the more I realize how much you are like him."

Positive patterns should be continued and negative ones discontinued. For example, from what I can learn, it has been a traditional pattern for men in my family to be reserved and uncommunicative about their feelings. I have had to learn to be open and free with my expressions of love and concern, and I am hopeful that my example will prevent that stoical tendency from being passed to my children.

3. The Gospel

Whether we are born into the gospel or discover it later on, its teachings can have a profound effect on us. The Spirit of the Holy Ghost and the teachings we receive in our homes and at church or seminary certainly influence how we view life and our goals and aspirations.

4. Our Own Choices

There are many things in life over which we have little control, such as the level of happiness or unhappiness in our parents' marriages. But there are many things over which you have great control. God has given us the marvelous gift of agency, but though we are free to choose our actions, we must also bear the consequences of our choices. The verses previously quoted (D&C 93:38–39) remind us that "the wicked one cometh and taketh away light and truth, through disobedience, from the children of men." No matter how much we would like to blame our parents for our weaknesses and shortcomings, many of the things that plague us are the result of choices we have made. We take such things into marriage, but through the Atonement of Jesus Christ and by obedience to the principles of his gospel, we can make substantial changes (see chapter 9).

5. The Significant People in Our Lives

Many of us, especially when we were teenagers, have done things we knew were not right or good for us as a result of peer pressure. But our friends and associates exert an influence on us, regardless of our age. Think about your life for a moment. Who are the people who have had a negative influence on you? Which ones have had a positive influence? Other significant people might include Church teachers and leaders, schoolteachers, employers, and close relatives. A seventh-grade teacher of mine had a most profound influence on my life. I will never forget him and how he helped me feel good about myself because he showed an interest in me.

6. Male/Female Differences

The fact that we are male or female means that we are inherently different in many ways, not only physically but also emotionally and temperamentally. It is simply true that men and women think and experience life differently. Commenting on these fundamental differences, Elder Spencer J. Condie used an analogy of a male and female musician seated together on a piano bench to play their first composition together: "The young woman fancies a rather soft and gentle treatment of the music, perhaps played with a mezzo-piano dynamics with a slow tempo. The young man envisions this composition as being played loud and fast. The fact of the matter is, women are not like men, and for that civilization can be eternally grateful. The refining, softening influence of women in the lives of children and families can scarcely be overemphasized."[4]

But having said that, it remains for a married couple to learn to accommodate each other in the areas where due to gender they are basically different. It is an ongoing challenge in any marriage.

7. Community

The place or places we are raised impact our outlook and values. A boy coming from a small farming town will certainly look at life differently than a girl raised in a large city. Someone raised in a wealthy environment will likely view things differently from someone raised in less-affluent circumstances.

8. Education

Certainly the years we have spent sitting in school classes and reading and studying books have an impact on who we are. Our teachers and coaches have also made an impression of one kind or another on us. Some of my university teachers caused me to think, evaluate, and decide on the course I wanted to pursue in life.

The impact these eight factors have on who we are might be illustrated as follows:

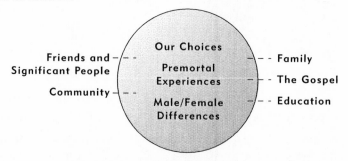

So how do we deal with such differences?

First, respect the agency of your partner and learn to be sensitive to gender differences. Recognize that some differences can be very positive factors in a relationship, providing wonderful balance in a marriage. Take, for example, a relationship where the man is energetic, impulsive, and assertive, and the woman is slower to act and more thoughtful. Certain benefits can come to the relationship when two different people with different strengths work together, complementing each other's efforts. In the previous example the woman might help the man be more cautious and take a careful look at situations before making decisions. At the same time, the man would perhaps assist the woman to become more organized and productive. There can be strength in diversity if couples respect each other and are willing to learn from each other. President Gordon B. Hinckley has said, "Recognize your differences. You will find that is a very wholesome and stimulating thing."[5]

Second, learn to be tolerant and forgiving of differences that cannot be resolved. Brother Truman Madsen related an experience he had with President Spencer W. Kimball, which also illuminates this point: "I once sat with [President Kimball] in a ticklish situation of marriage counseling. He drew two overlapping figures that were somewhat like circles, but the overlap in the center was a larger area than the two ends that didn't overlap. And his point was that differences—man, woman, husband, and wife—maybe are no-man's-lands or no-woman's-lands. These he and Camilla just never entered and learned not to try to. We should acknowledge that. That's an individual problem. Perhaps it will be resolved eventually, but when you find out that there are some areas in which you are just not overlapping, then endure them."[6]

Third, work in a mature way to resolve disruptive differences. Serious problems occur in a relationship when there are conflicts over major issues such as religion, values, or goals. If we do not learn to deal with these, they can lead to a breakup or divorce. Dr. Brent Barlow suggests that the following can happen:[7]

Differences- - ➤ Disagreements- - ➤ Conflict- - ➤ Anger - - ➤ Breakup or Divorce

Conflict and anger have a devastating impact on relationships. Hurt feelings, resentment, and a loss of the Spirit of the Lord usually result. In many marriages, the failure to manage anger is the number one cause of pain and unhappiness. Some differences are simply annoying and, by exercising patience, can be overlooked. Elder Spencer J. Condie emphasized this when he wrote: "The great plan of happiness provides countless opportunities for learning to resolve differences, to love, to tolerate and to forgive, and, in the process, to become more like our Heavenly Father and His Son. Opposition in all things, including marriage, does not have to include dissension and continual conflict, but rather the peaceable resolution of differences."[8] A useful exercise would be for you and your intended to select an area of concern that seems to be the most urgent and brainstorm together how each of you might make some changes. Then, because it takes willingness on the part of both parties to affect an improvement in a relationship, be willing to make some changes yourself.

Let me illustrate:

A young man I'll call John was seriously dating Jane. John felt he was in love with Jane and wanted to marry her. Jane, however, just couldn't make a commitment to marriage. Finally, John confronted her and said, "Why are you unwilling to get married? Is there something wrong with me?"

She replied, "No!"

"My family?"

Again, "No!"

"Then what's the problem?"

Finally, Jane admitted that she was worried that after marriage he might fall out of love with her. When John asked why she would be concerned about such a thing, Jane responded, "Because my father stopped loving my mother after many years of marriage."

The essential difference in this relationship was that John was willing to make a commitment and Jane was not. But they had reached an impasse. What could they do?

They both needed to give something. John would need to give Jane some time to build her level of trust, while further demonstrating his loyalty and devotion. For her part, Jane would need to sincerely pray about her feelings of mistrust and talk about them with her bishop in an effort to resolve them. She might also need some professional counseling to further assist her.

Many differences can be overcome if both partners are willing to make changes. But therein lies a most serious challenge. Let me illustrate. A colleague of mine, Dr. David H. Coombs, shared with me the following experience:

A couple who had been married for only six months came to him for counseling. The young woman was totally disillusioned by the way her husband treated her. He was verbally abusive and very insensitive to her. When the counselor asked the husband if that were true, he readily admitted it but defended himself by saying, "That's just the way I am."

David asked the wife, "Didn't you see this before you were married?"

Now, note her reply: "Yes, but I thought I could change him!"

The counselor then said, "What you get in courtship is what you get in marriage. If there are major problems before marriage, don't count on them going away after marriage. Any change needs to take place before marriage."

Couples need to learn how to resolve differences in a mature manner. I have adapted some points from Dr. William E. Hartman and called it "Ten Commandments for Resolving Conflicts in a Relationship."[9]

- Avoid attacking the person with such statements as, "You never . . ." or, "If you loved me . . ." Instead of *you*, use *we* and *us*. For example, "How can *we* improve our relationship?" "What is preventing *us* from communicating better?"
- Choose a time to discuss differences when both of you are psychologically ready. Immediately after someone has made a mistake is not a good time to bring up a problem. Having a prayer together and inviting the Spirit of the Lord often brings a more receptive mood.
- When offering criticism, include yourself as part of the problem. You probably won't be far from the truth by doing so. After all, it usually takes two to create a problem! For example, saying "I realize I'm partly to blame" or "I think I made a mistake here" softens the blow.
- Try to understand the other person's point of view. Listen carefully

and avoid becoming angry or making cutting or negative com-
ments, which shut down communication. President Hinckley has
counseled us: "Live the gospel. That is so important. That means a
lot of things. That means sacrifice in some circumstances. That
means love and appreciation and respect. That means self-
discipline. That means curbing your temper and your tongue and
being careful what you say because words can wound just as deeply
and just as seriously as can anything that inflicts bodily harm."[10]

- Speak in a quiet and calm voice. Again, President Hinckley has
said, "Another thing is a soft answer, keeping your voice down.
Don't lose your temper. Speak quietly. There will be differences
but don't get stirred up over them. Just be quiet and calm and
speak softly one to another."[11]

- Never criticize your partner in front of other people. This creates
resentment.

- If some change is desired, give the other person time to think
things through instead of pressing for an immediate commitment
or decision.

- Ask yourself why this situation bothers you so much. Maybe you
will find that some rethinking on your part is desirable.

- Give specific suggestions, if possible, as to how improvement can
be made. Be prepared to make changes yourself.

- Compliment or show appreciation for any aspect of the situation
that you can. Praise any effort on the part of another to listen or to
change. For example, "Thank you for listening to my concerns.
I'm so grateful we can work on this together."

Assignment

1. Decide what you consider essential areas that need to be agreed to in a
marriage relationship. Decide also those that are not critical.

2. Review again the "Ten Commandments for Resolving Conflicts in a
Relationship." Which of the "ten commandments" do you feel are the
most important? Which of them needs the greatest attention in your
relationship?

CHAPTER 19

Breaking Up without Breaking Down

"To everything there is a season, and a time to every purpose under the heaven: . . . a time to get, and a time to lose; A time to keep, and a time to cast away" (Ecclesiastes 3:1, 6).

A young woman sat in my office with tears streaming down her cheeks. Through her sobs she said, "John broke up with me today. I don't know what to do. I feel so empty inside, like someone close to me has died." Then, after a few moments, "I'll never date again!"

"Breaking up" is something most people will experience at least once in their lifetime. Some people, perhaps, will go through the trauma a number of times. The title of a popular song summed it up well: "Breaking Up Is Hard to Do." But when relationships reach a certain level of intensity there are only two alternatives: to marry or to break off the relationship. Breaking up can be a very good alternative for some relationships; in other instances, it might be the wrong thing to do. Elder Marvin J. Ashton made an important point when he said, "We must ever realize that being single will never be as painful as being married to the wrong person with wrong and selfish standards."[1] First, what are some common reasons people break up?

Looking for Perfection

A young man I know broke off an engagement with a fine Latter-day

Saint young woman because he felt she was not spiritual enough. I asked him what he meant by "not spiritual enough." He replied that she was not as enthusiastic about the gospel as he was. I tried to point out to him that some people show their enthusiasm for the gospel in different ways. Some are not outgoing and verbal about it, and I wondered if that wasn't the case with his former fiancée. I asked him if she possessed other qualities he was looking for in an eternal companion. He answered by saying that she had most of those he was looking for. I then pointed out that in many instances, people choose a mate as much on the basis of potential as current perfection.

The truth is that each of us takes imperfections into marriage. Some men remain single into their thirties or forties because they can't accept this notion. They are looking (in vain) for the perfect woman. Someone has written: "God help the man who won't marry until he finds a perfect woman, and God help him still more if he finds her."

The Fear of Making a Commitment

The word *commitment* strikes fear in the hearts of some people. The thought that they will have to give up the "single life" and commit to an eternal relationship is too much for some. The more serious the relationship becomes, the more uneasy they become.

A Desire to Date Another Person or Other People

Sometimes men and women delay marrying simply because they want to get to know other people. This may be particularly true for someone who has not dated very much.

Not Feeling Ready for Marriage

I have asked a lot of married couples if they felt they were ready for marriage. Most said they were not. If every couple who married waited until they were ready, there would be few marriages.

Losing Faith in Inspiration Once Received

I have known a number of young people who, after becoming

engaged, broke off the relationship because they doubted the inspiration they had received earlier. Elder Jeffrey R. Holland has cautioned young people to be careful with what they do with revelation they have been given: "Once there has been divine illumination, beware the temptation to retreat from a good thing. If it was right when you prayed about it and trusted it and lived for it, it is right now. Don't give up when the pressure mounts.

"After you have gotten a message, after you have paid the price to feel his love and hear the word of the Lord, 'go forward.' Don't fear, don't vacillate, don't quibble, don't whine. . . . God will provide the means and power to achieve that purpose. Trust in that eternal truth. If God has told you something is right, if something is indeed true for you, he will provide the way for you to accomplish it. That is true of joining the Church. It is true of getting an education, of going on a mission, or of getting married."[2]

It is not uncommon for relationships to plateau or to cease growing. When that happens, it is not necessarily the fault of either person. In some instances the relationship is not a good match. In other cases, one or both people may not be prepared for marriage and the sacrifices necessary to make it work. Remember, love is work!

Here are seven signs that a relationship might be in trouble.[3]

1. A feeling of being hemmed in

When one or both parties begin to feel that they do not have space to grow and progress, such a feeling may be an indication that the relationship has reached a plateau.

2. A feeling of being obligated

A growing relationship carries with it the feeling that we want to do things for the other person. When serving becomes a constant burden for us and we do things simply because we are expected to, we had better reevaluate the relationship.

3. Communication becomes strained

A growing relationship is based on the ability to communicate honestly, openly, and kindly with each other. When this ceases and irritability or anger enters the relationship, it will likely not develop much further.

4. Inappropriate or excessive physical involvement

Inappropriate physical involvement prior to marriage is often a factor in the death of a relationship. When that becomes the focus of the relationship, communication in other areas will usually stop. Feelings of guilt and/or resentment create stresses that destroy mutual respect and wholesome affection. Immorality also deprives the couple of the Spirit of the Lord in their relationship. Brother M. Gawain Wells has written: "A couple's physical attraction to one another may mask an inability to communicate. Some couples may know how to kiss but don't know how to talk to each other. For them, the physical aspect of their relationship is something they fall back on to avoid developing caring and communication."[4]

5. Increased conflict in the relationship

It is normal in growing relationships for couples to have occasional disagreements. However, when a relationship has stopped growing, conflicts will generally occur more frequently. This usually happens because we subconsciously realize that the relationship is not as enjoyable or fulfilling as it once was.

6. Dishonesty in the relationship

When one or both parties begin being dishonest, the relationship is definitely in trouble. This usually starts with little things, such as telling a lie about why we didn't call or why we didn't show up for an activity. This leads to a practice of not disclosing our real feelings.

7. A feeling that our needs are not being met

When we fall in love, we do so in part because someone meets our needs, but we all change, and often our needs change. People fall out of love because they change or their partner changes. This is the most common reason for a number of "Dear Johns" and "Dear Janes."

What can you do if you feel a relationship is not right?

First, do not prolong a relationship you feel isn't going anywhere. If you've already made up your mind to break it off, it isn't fair to the other person to try to sever the relationship slowly. It also isn't fair to pretend everything is okay or hope he or she figures it out. It is usually not a good idea, either, to say that you will remain best friends after you have broken up. I have rarely seen this work because sooner or later another boyfriend or girlfriend enters the picture.

Second, communicate your feelings in a sensitive and clear manner. At an appropriate time and place, explain to the one you have cared for that your feelings toward the relationship have changed. You cannot control the other person's reactions, but you can control when and how you share your feelings. Anger and accusations only create deep wounds and resentment.

How do you get over breaking up? Surviving an ended relationship is somewhat akin to surviving the death of a loved one. There needs to be a time of mourning and grieving—a time to recognize that the relationship is over. The pain can be very real and very intense; however, the hurt will eventually pass. President Hinckley has a motto: "Things work out, they always do."[5] So it is with ended relationships. You need to believe that things will be okay and will work out. You may feel as though you want to hide out, but it won't help to isolate yourself from others. It isn't useful, either, to be too critical of yourself.

The ultimate peace during these times comes from the Lord. How do we receive this peace? By intensifying our scripture study, our personal prayers, and our service to others. A priesthood blessing can also be a source of strength and provide hope and encouragement.

Another important thing is to get rid of things that constantly remind you of the relationship—such things as pictures or mementos. This may be difficult to do, but until they are gone, they will only serve to stir up the pain and prolong your suffering. Remember, the Lord wants you to be happy, and through these difficult times you will gain "experience" that will be for your good (see D&C 122:7).

How do you deal with breaking up if you felt you had a spiritual confirmation earlier that the relationship was right? Recognize that we sometimes misread spiritual confirmations. It is possible to want so much to be in love with someone that we convince ourselves it is right, in a sense providing our own answer to our prayers. In some cases the confirmation may mean that the relationship had potential or was good for the moment. The Lord may have been saying: "Yes, pursue this relationship; you will learn from it."

"Breaking up," as the song says, "*is* hard to do," but it can be a learning experience that will help you grow. The most important question you can ask is "What did I learn from this that will help me be better prepared when I finally meet the person I will marry?"

Assignment

If you have been in a relationship in the past, what did you learn about yourself from that experience? What did you learn about the qualities you would like in an eternal companion?

CHAPTER 20

Whom Shall You Marry?

"But, behold, I say unto you, that you must study it out in your mind; then you must ask me if it is right" (D&C 9:8).

Deciding whom you should marry is probably the biggest single decision you will ever make. President David O. McKay counseled that this decision should be entered into with great care. "The love of husband and wife is an eternal bond, not sealed lightly in frivolity or passion but entered into by premeditation, careful observation, sacred association and prayer."[1] For most couples, passion is the most immediate and compelling part of the relationship, but as President McKay counseled, the marriage decision must be made only after careful observation and thought, and couples need to consider a *number* of critical things that will affect their marriage.

President Spencer W. Kimball also emphasized the importance of making a sound decision: "The decision is not made on the spur of the moment. It is something you plan all your life. Certainly the most careful *planning,* and *thinking* and *praying* and *fasting* should be done to be sure that of all decisions, this one is not wrong."[2]

President Gordon B. Hinckley has added his thoughts on this subject, saying: "The most important decision of life is the decision concerning your companion. Choose prayerfully."[3]

Elder Bruce R. McConkie also had some strong feelings on this topic and offered this advice: "Well, do you want a wife? You go to work, you use the agency and power and ability that God has given you. You use every faculty and get all the judgment you can center on the problem, you make up your own mind and then, to be sure that you don't err, you counsel with the Lord. You talk it over. You say, 'I know what I think; what do you think?' And if you get the calm sweet surety that comes only from the Holy Spirit, you know you've reached the right conclusion; but if there's anxiety and uncertainty in your heart, then you'd better start over, because the Lord's hand is not in it and you're not getting the ratifying seal that, as a member of the Church who has the gift of the Holy Ghost, you are entitled to receive."[4]

How do you go about making such a decision? What criteria do you use to judge whether a person is someone you should marry? Here are five questions for you to consider:

Question 1: Are you basically compatible in the ten areas discussed in chapter 17?

Let's review each point and think about the positive and negative signals you will need to consider:

Area	Positive Signs	Danger Signs
Religion	You are both equally committed to the Church and gospel.	One or both of you are not committed to the Church and gospel.
Integrity/Honesty	Both have been open and honest in the relationship.	One or both of you have frequently lied.
Communication	You both share feelings and listen to each other.	You really don't share feelings.
Role Preferences	You feel comfortable with how you both perceive your roles.	You have unresolved differences about gender roles.
Family/Friends	You enjoy and like each other's family and friends.	Family and friends are a point of contention.

Conflict Resolution	You have been able to resolve conflict in a kind way.	You always fight about the same old things.
Financial Management	You both agree on how finances should be handled and both are committed to controlling spending.	One or both of you have a pattern of un-controlled spending.
Physical Intimacy/ Children	Physical intimacy has been kept within the bounds the Lord has set.	The focus of the relationship has been physical intimacy.
Personality/ Interests	You enjoy many activities together.	You have few common interests.
Goals	You share the same long-term goals.	You haven't discussed goals.

Question 2: Are you sufficiently in love to marry?

We have previously noted that love has three dimensions: romance, friendship, and the qualities of godliness. Both romantic love and friendship can be measured by the way we *feel* toward other people. Christlike love is manifest in the way we *behave* toward others. The type of love that will endure the challenges of marriage has to do with what you are willing to *do* for your partner and for God. Like a living plant, love must be nourished in order to grow and to bear fruit. Without the nourishment provided by mutual respect, a desire to serve and please each other, and a frequent dose of kindness and courtesy, love will wither and die. There is not sufficient nourishment in romance, no matter how passionate, to keep love alive if these other elements are not present.

In our culture, with its preoccupation with sex and romance, the marriage ceremony and the honeymoon are thought of as the culminating events in a relationship. This view might be diagrammed like this:

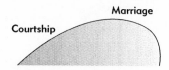

But from a gospel point of view, the marriage ceremony is only the beginning of a relationship where love will grow and mature throughout time and eternity! We could diagram the gospel view as follows:

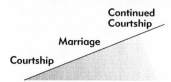

Speaking to a gathering of young people, President Spencer W. Kimball once reflected on how difficult marriage can be. He talked about the unique challenges newly married people face, and he told the group that once you are married and certain realities set in, the man or woman is no longer kept on a pedestal. Commenting on that talk, Brother Truman G. Madsen explained: "[President Kimball] warned them they were wrong if they expected that just the initial flash of romance and love would somehow perpetuate their marriage for the rest of their lives. No, they were going to have to go and get more and more of love, and then bring it home. And where do you get that? In the temple, for one place, and by serving each other and receiving the Spirit; the more you increase the Spirit, the more you increase in the power to love and be loved."[5]

What is love? Many people think of it as mere physical attraction, and they speak of "falling in love" and "love at first sight." This may be Hollywood's version and the interpretation of those who write love songs and love fiction. But true love is not wrapped in such flimsy material. Though one might become immediately attracted to another individual, true love is far more than a feeling of physical attraction. It is deep, inclusive, and comprehensive.

In an article addressed to those who are contemplating marriage, President Kimball said this: "The love of which the Lord speaks is not only physical attraction, but spiritual attraction as well. It is faith and confidence in, and understanding of one another. It is a total partnership with common ideals and standards. It is unselfishness toward and sacrifice for one another. It is cleanliness of thought and action and faith in God and his program. . . . This kind of love never tires or wanes. It lives on through sickness and sorrow, through prosperity and privation, through accomplishment and disappointment, through time and eternity. . . .

"For your love to ripen so gloriously, there must be an increase of confidence and understanding, a frequent and sincere expression of appreciation of one another. There must be a focusing of interests and hopes and objectives into a single channel."[6]

What can we learn about love from this? Let's look at four characteristics of true love, as described by President Kimball.

1. Faith, confidence, understanding, and partnership

An enduring love inspires within us those qualities that are the essence of true friendship. The opposite characteristics are jealousy and disharmony.

2. Great devotion and companionship

The person we love is our other half; they make us whole, and without them we are not complete. Because of this, we are naturally devoted to that person and take delight in serving them.

3. Cleanliness, sacrifice, and selflessness

The opposite of these is selfishness, often expressed in infidelity and immoral behavior. When a man and a woman are absolutely true to each other, their love has an environment where it can grow and flourish. True love, the kind of which eternal marriages are made, also has as one of its characteristics a willingness to sacrifice our own comfort or desires to ensure the happiness of our mate. Selfishness truly is at the root of most problems in relationships.

4. Forgetting self and demonstrating a constant concern for the other

The secret of a happy marriage is to give more than you receive. Real love, not the usual Hollywood kind, is not turned inward but outward. It constantly asks the question, "What can I do to assist my loved one to grow and to be happy?" One of my students described this impulse by saying, "It becomes instinctive to do things for the one you love. You just know what makes them happy, and wanting to add to their happiness is just a part of you."

Contrast these characteristics of love with the purely romantic view.

Romantic View

- Walking on the beach hand-in-hand at sunset.
- Sitting on the couch in front of a glowing fire, kissing.
- Listening to romantic music by candlelight.
- Being adored by your loved one, who is attentive to your every need.

Is that love? Yes, but only one dimension of it. A relationship based on romantic love alone, as stated earlier, will never endure the challenges of marriage.

Realistic View

Now, let's look at love from another point of view—the kind of love that delights in serving your partner. If you want to know if you are really in love, ask yourself these questions. Can you picture yourself:

- Working out a budget with the one you love, deciding what you will sacrifice to avoid going into debt.
- Being with this person when he is not as handsome or she not as beautiful, due to illness, injury, or advancing age.
- Staying up all night to care for this person because he or she is sick.
- Having a heartrending conversation with your partner—sharing your innermost thoughts and feelings on a difficult subject.
- Sharing household responsibilities, such as child rearing, cooking, cleaning, paying bills, and taking out the garbage.
- Growing old together.

These two contrasting views of marriage came to my mind when one of my students shared with me her feelings about a boy she was dating. The conversation went something like this:

"I really like him and think that maybe he's the one."

"What makes you think so?"

"I love him."

"What makes you think you love him?"

"I'm really attracted to him."

"Can I ask you a few questions?"

"Sure."

"Are you keeping the standards of the gospel?"

"Not really."

"What do you mean?"

"Well, we're having some morality problems."

"Have you been to see your bishop?"

"No."

"Do the two of you sacrifice for each other?"

"What do you mean?"

"Do you exercise self-control, and are you kind and sensitive to each other?"

"Well, lately, we fight a lot."

"Do you share your innermost feelings with each other?"

"Well, I do. But he's not willing to open up to me."

"Do you make time to really listen to each other?"

"We don't seem to do much together that's fun anymore. We used to do fun things and talk and listen to each other."

"So what do you do now?"

"Mostly watch TV and kiss a lot."

"So, what makes you think you're in love?"

"I'm attracted to him!"

Do you see the problem here? Physical attraction alone, without the impulse to sacrifice and serve the other person, is not enough on which to build a solid, enduring marriage. Love is more about giving than it is receiving. So are you in love enough to get married?

Question 3: Does your relationship have all three dimensions of true love—friendship, romance, and Christlike love?

One college-age young woman told me she was having trouble choosing between two young men she had been dating. Both had proposed marriage to her, and she couldn't make up her mind which proposal to accept. I suggested she evaluate her two suitors on the basis of the three dimensions of love—romantic (physical); friendship (social, intellectual, and emotional); and Christlike (spiritual), by answering the following questions with respect to each young man:

Romance—"Do you feel attracted to and do you want to be attractive for him?" She responded by saying that she felt about the same for each of them.

Friendship—"Do you enjoy being with him, and do you have a lot of things in common?" Again she replied that it was about the same for each of them.

"Do you have similar intellectual pursuits, and do you communicate on the same intellectual level?" Again she replied that it was about the same for each young man.

"Can you trust him with your innermost feelings, and does he trust you with his? Is he your best friend? Can you picture him as the father of your children?" Here she noted a slight difference between the young men. She said she was more comfortable sharing her feelings with one of them and felt she had a closer *friendship* with him.

Christlike feelings—"Does he inspire you to want to be the very best person you can become? Does this relationship motivate you to want to draw closer to your Heavenly Father? Do you desire to serve and love your friend no matter what the challenges might be?"

Then I read to her a wonderful statement by President David O. McKay: "Well, you may ask, 'How may I know when I am in love?' That is a very important question. A fellow student and I considered that query one night as we walked together. As boys of that age frequently do, we were talking of girls. Neither he nor I knew whether or not we were in love. Of course, I had not then met my present sweetheart. In answer to my question, 'How may we know when we are in love?' he replied: 'My mother once said that if you meet a girl in whose presence you feel a desire to achieve, who inspires you to do your best, and to make the most of yourself, such a young woman is worthy of your love and is awakening love in your heart.'"[7]

This brought to the young woman's mind a major difference between the two young men. "With one," she said, "I feel a spiritual bond between us and Heavenly Father. I can picture myself loving him and sacrificing for him forever."

Elder Richard G. Scott described this kind of love by saying, "Love, as defined by the Lord, elevates, protects, respects, and enriches another. It motivates one to make sacrifices for another."[8]

She had her answer.

Question 4: Are you committed to keeping your marriage covenants?

Being married in the temple involves making sacred covenants. You and your loved one must be absolutely committed to keeping those promises. How can you gauge your level of commitment? Reflect on the covenants you have already made. Have you been true and faithful to your baptismal covenants? Have the two of you kept yourselves worthy and clean during your dating experience? Does being together promote faith and obedience, or are the two of you bad for each other in this regard?

Question 5: Have the two of you ever made a decision together and then fasted and prayed to receive the Lord's confirmation?

Speaking to an audience of young men, President Ezra Taft Benson said: "Do not be so particular [in choosing a wife] that you overlook her most important qualities of having a strong testimony, living the principles of the gospel, loving home, wanting to be a mother in Zion, and supporting you in your priesthood responsibilities.

"Of course, she should be attractive to you, but do not just date one girl after another for the sole pleasure of dating without seeking the Lord's confirmation in your choice of your eternal companion.

"And one good yardstick as to whether a person might be the right one for you is this: in her presence, do you think your noblest thoughts, do you aspire to your finest deeds, do you wish you were better than you are?"[9]

My experience has been that when we ask the Lord to confirm our choice of a companion, the answer seldom comes in the form of a dramatic spiritual experience. Though there are instances where this has happened, such answers usually come in the form of a peaceful, calm feeling or a warm sense of well-being.

Such an experience is sweet. I shall always remember my own feelings when Susan and I sat together in an empty chapel, and I asked her to marry me. Every signal indicated she was the one for me. She inspired me to want to be my very best, and I wanted to do everything I could do to make her happy.

True love, with all its elements in place, might be compared to a beautiful piece of piano music. When the relationship is right the music is beautiful and pleasing and there is a sense of harmony among you, the one you love, and your Heavenly Father.

By following this pattern of marrying in the temple and keeping the covenants you have made, the love you feel for your eternal companion will grow and deepen through the years of mortality and into eternity.

Assignment

If you are wondering if you are in love, ask yourself these questions:

- Are you obeying the commandments and living the gospel fully?

- Are you trying to do your best?

- Do you feel as though this person is your best friend?

- Do you respect this person?

- Will this person assist you in progressing toward your ultimate goals in life, especially your spiritual goals?

- Does he or she inspire you to want to reach your full potential?

- Are you prepared to keep your marriage vows no matter what problems or challenges may confront you?

- Have you fasted and prayed together to receive the Lord's confirmation of your decision?

- Do you feel a sense of peace and well-being when you think about this person, or are you unsettled in your mind and somewhat anxious about how to proceed? If you are unsettled, have you counseled with your parents and/or your bishop about this relationship?

CHAPTER 21

Temple Courtship

"Organize yourselves; prepare every needful thing"
(D&C 88:119).

Marriage is such a lofty, time-honored, and sacred institution that, for me, it is a disturbing thing that so many couples in today's world simply begin living together. Among those in the world who do legally formalize their union, the emphasis is usually on planning the details of the ceremony, the reception, and the honeymoon. But for Latter-day Saints—those desiring to achieve an *eternal* marriage—there is another, more important consideration: planning and preparing to go to the holy temple.

That is the reason I entitled this chapter "Temple Courtship." Courtship refers to that period of time when a couple is dating each other exclusively and seriously exploring the possibility of getting married. When that decision has been made, the engagement usually occurs. This is an exciting time for a couple, but it can also be a time filled with extraordinary activity and stress. In the midst of all this, the couple needs to prepare themselves for the spiritual experience they will have in the temple as well as to keep themselves worthy. Of these often hectic preparations, Elder Richard G. Scott has said, "Do not let receptions, wedding breakfasts, or other activities overshadow the sacred temple experience."[1] Here are five areas to consider in this serious period of a relationship:

1. Prepare spiritually for your temple experience.

The better prepared you are for the ordinances of the temple, the greater the likelihood you will appreciate them. There are a number of things you can do to prepare for these ordinances:

- Read a book written specifically about the temple. See the bibliography provided in this book.
- Meet with your bishop about the temple and be receptive to his counsel and direction.
- Take a temple preparation class. This can be arranged through your ward, stake, or institute of religion.
- Study carefully the book of Moses in the Pearl of Great Price and Section 109 of the Doctrine and Covenants, which is the prayer offered by Joseph Smith at the dedication of the Kirtland Temple.
- Talk as a couple about how you will make the temple central to your relationship after you are married.
- Review the clothing in your wardrobe to make sure it is appropriate once you have received your endowment and begin wearing the garment of the holy priesthood. Discard or give away those articles you will not be able to use.
- Pray for the ability to understand the temple ceremony and to be sensitive to the special spirit there.

2. Confirm the dates and times for the temple ordinances.

If possible, you may want to receive the endowment a few days before your temple sealing so that sufficient attention can be given to this important and sacred ordinance. In regard to this, Elder Richard G. Scott has counseled: "The endowment and sealing ordinances of the temple are so gloriously rich in meaning that you will want to allow significant time to receive those ordinances and to ponder their meaning. You may want to divide them into two temple visits. On your first visit, if possible, take an endowed member of your family or a close friend of your own gender to escort you."[2]

3. Discuss important areas of marriage.

Each of us takes into marriage a "script" of how we imagine marriage will be. The young man has tried to picture himself as a husband and his bride as a wife. The young woman has some concept of herself as a wife and her young man as a husband. Courtship is a time to discuss these "scripts" and to make important decisions. It is much easier to come to an agreement on essential issues before marriage than after. Though it is difficult to imagine exactly how things will go once you are married, these are some areas you might discuss:

- Living the gospel—What about Church attendance, the payment of tithing, accepting callings, family prayer, and temple attendance?
- Children—How many children do we want? How will we divide parental responsibilities? What will we do to ensure that our relationship continues to grow after the birth of children?
- Finances—How much debt will we each bring into our marriage? How will we pay the debt off and stay debt free? Will we have a budget? Who will pay the bills and balance the checkbook?
- Roles—How will we handle or divide household tasks, meal preparation, car maintenance, home repairs, yard work, washing and ironing clothes? Who will take the lead in spiritual matters such as family prayer, family home evening, and family scripture study?
- Priorities—What will we do to keep our marriage one of our top priorities so that jobs, friends, and other interests don't take on a greater importance?
- Decision making—How will we maintain unity in our relationship when it comes to making important decisions?

4. Make preparations for the reception and honeymoon.

Some couples experience great stress and sometimes contention during the planning of the reception and honeymoon. You must realize that the two mothers have dreamed and even planned for your wedding longer than you have, at least since you were a child. Though you need to be sensitive to the input of others (budgets, etc.), remember, this is *your* wedding. Here are some things you might consider:

- Provide enough time between your temple sealing and wedding breakfast or the reception so that you can give full attention to each.
- Obtain and use a checklist that will help you outline in detail what needs to be done for the reception. Such a list can be found in most bridal magazines.
- Define clearly at an early stage of the planning which responsibilities the groom's parents will have and which the bride's parents will have.
- Should you have two receptions, space them out if possible.
- Be sensitive to the financial capabilities of your parents. Even if they aren't lavish, wedding receptions—and honeymoons—are generally expensive. Be reasonable and practical as you make your plans. If you work or have a savings account, you may want to help out your parents financially.

5. Decide together that you will immediately become a separate family of your own.

Elder Boyd K. Packer gives the following advice to couples that he is asked to seal in the temple: "First of all, today, as you are sealed for time and for all eternity, you become a separate family on the records of the Church, and that is a separation in a very real sense. All of the ties that have bound you to your father and mother to this point we undo today. We untie them all. . . . Many of them we leave permanently untied. That is why your mothers will be crying today . . . because they know, in a very real sense, that they are losing and that they should lose you as you become a separate family on the records of the Church."[3]

You should discuss together what you will do to maintain your own separate family unit. It would be well, also, to make a commitment that there will be no running home to parents if there are problems: resolve to solve them together.

The courtship period of a relationship can and should be a wonderful time filled with anticipation and exciting events. But don't let all of that divert your attention from the most important thing of all—your temple ordinances and the sealing ceremony. Remember, too, that temple courtship does not end with the ceremony; it should continue through your mortal time on earth and on into eternity. You will always want to be kind, sensitive, and thoughtful throughout your married life. And you will want to center your marriage on the holy temple. That is true temple courtship!

Assignment

Read and discuss together the following scriptures:

- Proverbs 15:1
- Romans 12:10,16
- Ephesians 5:25–33
- D&C 38:27
- D&C 121:41–46

CHAPTER 22

The Holy Temple

"Search diligently, pray always, and be believing, and all things shall work together for your good, if ye walk uprightly and remember the covenant wherewith ye have covenanted one with another" (Doctrine and Covenants 90:24).

The very key to an eternal marriage is the holy temple and the covenants you make therein. The word *covenant* is not new to you. You have been taught about the importance of your baptismal covenants and how these are renewed during the sacrament. Baptism and the sacrament are ordinances of the gospel that are administered by the priesthood. Elder John A. Widtsoe, a former member of the Quorum of the Twelve Apostles, defined an ordinance. Look for the three characteristics of an ordinance in Elder Widtsoe's description: "An ordinance is an earthly symbol of a spiritual reality. It is usually also an act of symbolizing a covenant or agreement with the Lord. Finally, it is nearly always an act in anticipation of a blessing from heaven. An ordinance, then, is distinctly an act that connects heaven and earth, the spiritual and the temporal."[1] Did you note the three characteristics of ordinances?

1. An ordinance is a physical act that symbolizes a spiritual reality.

For example, the physical act of baptism represents both death (of the "old" man being "buried" in the water), and birth (of the "new" man emerging from the water into a newness of life through Jesus Christ).

2. An ordinance involves making covenants.

Each ordinance has as its central focus a covenant or covenants. A covenant is a solemn agreement between God and man. Contracts are agreements between mortals. The problem with mortal contracts is that each partner is human and may default on the agreement. This is not so with God; he will always fulfill his part and has told us so in no uncertain terms: "I, the Lord, am bound when ye do what I say; but when ye do not what I say, ye have no promise" (D&C 82:10). Therefore, the realization of any promised blessing depends on us keeping our part of the covenant. The relationship of ordinances and covenants might be diagrammed as follows:

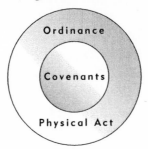

3. An ordinance provides blessings we can anticipate as we keep our covenants.

Let's review these three elements of ordinances by looking at three ordinances with which you are probably very familiar: baptism, the sacrament, and (for the young men) ordination to the Melchizedek Priesthood.

The Physical Act	Our Covenant	Anticipated Blessings
Baptism— We are buried in water and come forth into a newness of life	To always remember Christ and keep his commandments. Also to mourn with those that mourn and stand as witnesses of God at all times and in all places (see Mosiah 18:10).	Forgiveness of sin and reception of the Holy Ghost.

The Physical Act	Our Covenant	Anticipated Blessings
Sacrament—We partake of the bread and water, symbolically taking Christ and his teachings into our lives.	To always remember Christ and to keep his commandments.	We will always have his Spirit to be with us.
Ordination to the Melchizedek Priesthood—Hands are laid upon the head of the recipient.	That the bearer will magnify his calling.	All that the Father has will be given him.

By keeping the covenants made at baptism and by renewing those covenants by partaking worthily of the sacrament, we have our sins remitted and receive the Holy Ghost in preparation for one day entering the celestial kingdom. By honoring his priesthood covenant, a young man prepares himself to be a worthy missionary and husband and father and qualifies himself to enter the holy temple. By honoring her baptismal covenant, a young woman prepares herself to be a worthy handmaiden of the Lord, a wife, and a mother and also qualifies herself to enter the holy temple.

To inherit eternal life we need to receive ordinances that are administered only in the house of the Lord. President Gordon B. Hinckley taught the significance of these sacred ceremonies by saying: "The gospel is not complete, it is only partly here without the ordinances of the House of the Lord, and in order to complete our acceptance of the Church it is necessary that we have this holy house. Let every man and woman . . . resolve that you will come to the House of the Lord."[2]

Two of these ordinances are the endowment and the sealing of husbands and wives to each other. "The endowment," wrote Elder John A. Widtsoe, "given to members of the Church in the temples falls into several divisions. First, there is a course of instruction relative to man's eternal journey from the dim beginning towards his possible glorious destiny. Then, conditions are set up by which that endless journey may be upward in direction. Those who receive this information covenant to obey the laws of eternal progress, and thereby give life to the knowledge received. Finally, it is made clear that a man must sometimes give an account of his deeds, and prove the possession of divine knowledge and religious works. It is a very beautiful, logical and inspiring series of ceremonies."[3]

You are probably more familiar with the sealing (marriage) ordinance than you are with the endowment. Sometimes young people go to the temple to be sealed without realizing how very important the endowment ordinance is. The sealing ordinance is based on the endowment, and while sealing is the crowning ordinance, the endowment is equally important.

Each time I attend the temple and participate in the endowment ordinance I try to remember that I am participating in a symbolic representation of a journey from the premortal life, through mortality, back to the presence of God. This is the symbolism of the physical act of the endowment. Central to the endowment are the associated covenants we make with the Lord. Elder James E. Talmage described these covenants as follows:

"The ordinances of the endowment embody certain obligations on the part of the individual, such as covenant and promise to observe the law of strict virtue and chastity, to be charitable, benevolent, tolerant and pure; to devote both talent and material means to the spread of truth and the uplifting of the race; to maintain devotion to the cause of truth; and to seek in every way to contribute to the great preparation that the earth may be made ready to receive her King,— the Lord Jesus Christ. With the taking of each covenant and the assuming of each obligation a promised blessing is pronounced, contingent upon the faithful observance of the conditions."[4]

The anticipated blessing associated with the endowment ordinance is that we will one day return to God's presence, pure and clean. The sealing ordinance is the only ordinance I know of that involves more than the person receiving it and the Lord. In the case of families being sealed it involves parents and their children. In the case of marriage, it involves the couple and the Lord. The physical act of kneeling at an altar in the temple has great spiritual significance. In Old Testament times, it was at an altar where the priest would offer a sacrificial animal as a symbol of the sacrifice of Jesus

Christ. In the temple marriage ceremony, a couple kneel across from each other at an altar. Then, holding hands, the two are put under covenant to each other and to the Lord. Thus, they are reminded by the ceremony to center their marriage on the teachings and sacrifice of Jesus Christ. They also covenant to be faithful to each other, to keep the covenants they have made with the Lord, and to raise their children in righteousness.

Emphasizing the importance of this sacred ordinance, Elder Bruce R. McConkie has written: "Celibacy is not of God, whose law is that 'Marriage is honourable in all' (Heb. 13:4), and that men should 'Be fruitful, and multiply, and replenish the earth.' (Gen. 1:28.)"[5]

Normal men and women of adult age should marry if they have proper opportunity so to do. To deliberately refrain from assuming marital or parental obligation is to fail the most important test of this mortal probation. The whole plan of salvation and exaltation centers in and revolves around the family unit. 'Whoso forbiddeth to marry is not ordained of God, for marriage is ordained of God unto man.' (D&C 49:15.)

Quoting Elder McConkie again: "The most important things that any member of The Church of Jesus Christ of Latter-day Saints ever does in this world are: 1) To marry the right person, in the right place, by the right authority; and 2) To keep the covenant made in connection with this holy and perfect order of matrimony—thus assuring the obedient persons of an inheritance of exaltation in the celestial kingdom."[6]

Often young people ask, "How can I prepare for the temple?" My answer is usually the same: "Strive to keep your baptismal covenants, which means keeping the commandments and serving faithfully in Church callings." To young men I add, "Keep the covenant you made when you received the priesthood." Then, when you go to the temple, pay particular attention to the covenants you make with the Lord. They are the keys to eternal life. Elder Boyd K. Packer emphasized this when he wrote:

"The word *ordinance* means, 'a religious or ceremonial observance'; 'an established rite.' The *Oxford English Dictionary* gives as the first definition of the word *order*, 'arrangements in ranks or rows,' and as the second definition, 'arrangement in sequence or proper relative position.' At first glance that may not strike a person as having much religious significance, but indeed it has."[7]

Order your life after the covenants the Lord has offered you. The covenants you make with the Lord are what he requires of you in order that you might receive eternal life. Only in the holy temple can you receive these covenants, the highest of which is the sealing of man and woman in marriage for time and for all eternity.

I have found that many of our young people do not understand the significance of what it means to be "sealed." They think of it as two people being "fastened or attached" together by God for all eternity. Another meaning of "seal" goes back to ancient times when a king or queen would impress his or her seal or mark of authenticity in wax on an agreement. This is much closer to the meaning of "seal" as used in temple marriages. As the husband and wife keep their covenants, God, through the Holy Spirit, places his stamp of approval on the eternal character of that marriage relationship. This means that the love you have for your companion can last forever. Indeed, as Elder Boyd K. Packer has said, temple marriage is only the beginning:

"I picture you coming to the temple to be sealed for time and for all eternity. I yearn to talk to you about the sacred sealing ordinance, but this we do not do outside those sacred walls. The transcendent nature of all that is conferred upon us at the marriage altar is so marvelous it is worth all the waiting and all of the resisting. I picture you, as I have seen you often. The young man, masculine, clear of vision, stalwart of frame, firm to accept the responsibilities as a husband and as a father. And the bride, unassuming, beautifully feminine, an inspiration to her sweetheart, and dependent on him.

"But this is not the fulfillment of the story of love. In the book, or the play, on the stage, the curtain comes down here. But it is not so in real love. This is not the conclusion—only the beginning. . . . This picture, then I see, and were I an artist, had I the power, I would paint this picture over and over again—not with oil or canvas or brush, but with counsel and admonition and encouragement and blessing, with forgiveness and reassurance, with the truth. . . . The exalted concepts of marriage and of courtship and of romantic love [as taught in The Church of Jesus Christ of Latter-day Saints is that they] are ordained of God. . . . Love is a promise and there is a Holy Spirit of Promise. I cannot frame this picture—I would not if I could for there are no bounds. Love like this may have a beginning, but never through all eternity need it have an end."[8]

Assignment

1. What is the significance of ordinances to you? What blessings can be yours should you choose to "order" your life after the ordinances of the priesthood?

2. Carefully examine how well you are keeping the covenants you have already made with the Lord. These covenants are the measuring rod as to how well prepared you are for the holy temple.

Section 4 Summary Points

1. Successful dating is dating that helps you prepare to one day marry in the temple.

2. The standard works and our Church leaders have provided guidelines to protect you during your dating years.

3. You will likely marry someone you date or associate with.

4. Marry someone who has similar values, interests, and goals.

5. You need to choose the person you will marry through planning, prayer, and fasting.

6. Learning to deal with and appreciate differences in your marriage partner is the key to building a happy marriage.

7. Breaking up, for all its pain, can be a useful learning experience.

8. Courtship is a time to focus on preparing to go to the holy temple.

9. The temple ordinances offer us an opportunity to make sacred covenants, which, if we are faithful, make it possible for us to attain eternal life with our family.

Conclusion

Writing this book has been one of the most wonderful experiences of my life, and yet it has been one of the most challenging. Putting into words the feelings and experiences I have had with hundreds of young people has not been easy. And the subjects we have discussed—dating, love, courtship, and marriage—are not always easy to define and to describe. But then, I shouldn't feel alone. One of our prophets admitted that the subject of marriage was beyond his grasp. It was President Brigham Young who said:

"But the whole subject of the marriage relation is not in my reach, nor in any other man's reach on this earth. It is without beginning of days or end of years; it is a hard matter to reach. We can tell some things with regard to it; it lays the foundation for worlds, for angels, and for the Gods; for intelligent beings to be crowned with glory, immortality, and eternal lives. In fact, it is the thread which runs from the beginning to the end of the holy Gospel of salvation—of the Gospel of the Son of God; it is from eternity to eternity."[1]

That is grand stuff to contemplate. When I knelt at the altar with Susan, I certainly had no idea how important that event was to be in my life. Now, many years later, I think I am just beginning to catch a glimpse of the eternal significance of our decision to marry in the holy temple.

I hope it has been made amply clear that whom you will marry is the most important decision you will make in your lifetime. For this reason, I asked you in the very first chapter to consider what kind of marriage you want. If you desire, as I hope you do, a celestial marriage, then you will begin preparing yourself to marry the right person in the right place. The most important area of preparation is your personal relationship with your Heavenly Father and his Son, Jesus Christ. The mission of the Church is to "invite all to come unto Christ" (D&C 20:59). You come to him by keeping the covenants you made at baptism and through the ordinances of the holy temple. These covenants must not be taken lightly, for the Lord has said, "I will prove you in all things, whether you will abide in my covenant, even unto death, that you may be found worthy" (D&C 98:14). As you keep covenants, you will come to understand more deeply what perfect, or complete, love is. You will understand why romance, friendship, and Christlike love are important in marriage. And you will desire to keep romantic love within the bounds the Lord has set.

I asked you to also consider another question as you find yourself in a serious relationship: "Am I in love enough to marry?" One of the most important factors in answering this question is whether this relationship inspires you to love and serve your Heavenly Father.

I also asked you to evaluate if you were prepared to take on the challenges and demands of marriage—physical, mental, emotional, spiritual, and financial.

The final section, "Choosing for Eternity," ended with a chapter entitled "The Holy Temple." The decisions you are making right now regarding whom you date, the places you go on your dates, and the activities you engage in are either leading you toward or away from the temple. My testimony to you is that kneeling at the altar in the holy temple with the one you love and have chosen is worth every sacrifice, every effort you can make. For it is in the holy temple that you begin a celestial marriage, a marriage that will last forever.

President Spencer W. Kimball has summarized what it takes to find true happiness in marriage. Perhaps we can do no better in closing this narrative than quote his inspired words:

"If two people love the Lord more than their own lives and then love each other more than their own lives, working together in total harmony with the gospel program as their basic structure, they are sure to have this great happiness. When a husband and wife go together frequently to the holy temple, kneel in prayer together in their home with their family, go hand in hand to their religious meetings, keep their lives wholly chaste, mentally and physically, so that their whole thoughts and desires and love are all centered in one being, their companion, and both are working together for the upbuilding of the kingdom of God, then happiness is at its pinnacle."[2]

My sincere prayer is that you will follow the teachings of the holy scriptures and our Church leaders and receive every blessing our Heavenly Father has in store for you.

Selected Bibliography

Barlow, Brent A. *Dealing with Differences in Marriage*. Salt Lake City: Deseret Book, 1993.

——. *Just for Newlyweds*. Salt Lake City: Deseret Book, 1992.

Brinley, Douglas E., and Daniel K. Judd, ed. *Eternal Companions*. Salt Lake City: Bookcraft, 1995.

Broderick, Carlfred. *Couples: How to Confront Problems and Maintain Loving Relationships*. New York: Simon and Schuster, 1979.

——. *One Flesh, One Heart: Putting Celestial Love into Your Temple Marriage*. Salt Lake City: Deseret Book, 1986.

Bytheway, John. *What I Wish I'd Known When I Was Single*. Salt Lake City: Deseret Book, 1999.

Christensen, Joe J. *One Step at a Time: Building a Better Marriage, Family, and You*. Salt Lake City: Deseret Book, 1996.

Gottman, John M., and Nan Silver. *The Seven Principles for Making Marriage Work*. Lake Jackson, Texas: Crown Publishing, 1999.

Packer, Boyd K. *You May Claim the Blessings of the Holy Temple*. Salt Lake City: Bookcraft, 1980.

Skidmore, Rex A. *A Temple Marriage to Last Forever*. Salt Lake City: Bookcraft, 1991.

Wilcox, Michael S. *House of Glory: Finding Personal Meaning in the Temple*. Salt Lake City: Deseret Book, 1995.

Chapter Notes

Introduction

1. "Some Enchanted Evening," from *South Pacific*.

2. Joe J. Christensen, *One Step at a Time: Building a Better Marriage, Family, and You*. 1996, 35–36.

Chapter 1—What Kind of Marriage Do You Want?

1. *Mormon Doctrine*, 2d ed. 1966, 118.

2. *Marriage*. 1978, 31.

3. From a personal experience with Elder LeGrand Richards, 13 Dec. 1963.

4. "Priesthood and Partnerships: Some Thoughts for LDS Marriages," in *Association of Mormon Counselors and Psychotherapists*. Vol. 16, no. 1, 134–35; hereafter cited as AMCAP.

5. Ibid., 142.

6. "A Union of Love and Understanding," *Ensign*, Oct. 1994, 51.

7. *Your Agency: Handle with Care*. 1996, 113.

Chapter 2—Marriage and Your Plan of Happiness

1. *History of the Church*, 5:134–35.

2. Ibid.

3. *The Miracle of Forgiveness*. 1969, 236.

Chapter 3—Six Popular Marriage Myths

1. *The Radiant Life*. 1994, 90.

2. *The Way to Perfection*. 1975, 44–45.

3. As quoted in "I Have a Question," *Ensign*, June 1977, 40.

4. *The Teachings of Spencer W. Kimball*. 1982, 306.

5. "Revelation," in *Brigham Young University 1981–82 Fireside and Devotional Speeches*, 25.

6. "The Odyssey to Happiness," in *Speeches of the Year: BYU Devotional*

and Ten-Stake Fireside Addresses, 1974. 1975, 325.

7. *Eternal Love.* 1973, 11.

8. *To Draw Closer to God.* 1997, 7.

9. As quoted in "The Issue: Starting out Right in Marriage," *Centered on Families*, The Center for Studies of the Family, Summer 1997, [published by the Center for Family Studies, Provo, Utah: BYU], 15.

Chapter 4—The Law of the Harvest

1. *The Teachings of Ezra Taft Benson.* 1988, 532.

2. *Becoming Men and Women of Truth and Virtue* (CES fireside for young adults, 13 Sept. 1998), 1.

3. In Conference Report, Apr. 1956, 6.

4. *Ensign*, Nov. 1978, 105.

5. *The Teachings of Howard W. Hunter.* 1997, 73–74.

Chapter 5—Prepare Yourself Physically and Socially

1. *One Step at a Time*, 125.

2. Ibid.

3. *Eternal Love*, 9–10.

4. *The Teachings of Spencer W. Kimball*, 295–96.

5. As quoted in "Inner Confidence," *Church News*, 25 Oct. 1997, 15.

6. Adapted from *Update.* 1981, 29–30.

Chapter 6—Becoming Mentally and Emotionally Mature

1. "The Issue: Starting out Right in Marriage," *Centered on Families*, Summer 1997, 4.

2. "A Proper Orientation on the Threshold of Life," *Brigham Young University Speeches of the Year* (17 Jan. 1962), 8.

3. *Growing Up Emotionally.* 1957, 21.

4. In Conference Report, Apr. 1978, 140.

5. "Parenting and Adolescents," *Centered on Families*, Spring 1998, 10.

6. Ibid.

7. *The Teachings of Spencer W. Kimball*, 272.

8. *Ensign*, May 1994, 9.

Chapter 7—Learning to Be Unselfish

1. *The Teachings of Spencer W. Kimball*, 313.

2. "Hinckleys to Note 60th Anniversary," *Church News*, 19 Apr. 1997, 3.

3. *That My Family Should Partake.* 1974, 35–36.

4. In Conference Report, Apr. 1956, 9; or *Improvement Era*, June 1956, 396.

5. *Ensign*, May 1979, 72.

6. *Ensign*, May 1989, 4.

7. In Conference Report, Oct. 1954, 16.

8. *Ensign*, May 1991, 73.

9. *Ensign*, May 1979, 73.

10. Ibid.

11. *That My Family Should Partake*, 35–36.

Chapter 8—Make the Lord Your First Priority

1. *Gospel Ideals*. 1976, 390.

2. *Radiant Life*, 101–2.

3. *The Teachings of Ezra Taft Benson*, 350.

4. See Conference Report, Oct. 1961, 60–61; or *Improvement Era*, Dec. 1961, 947–48.

5. *Ensign*, May 1979, 25.

Chapter 9—Change What You Can Change

1. *Ensign*, Nov. 1985, 6.

2. *Ensign*, May 1990, 74–75.

3. In Conference Report, Apr. 1901, 63.

4. "A Mighty Change of Heart," *Ensign*, Oct. 1989, 5.

5. *The Miracle of Forgiveness*, 176.

Chapter 10—Love: Fact and Fiction

1. *The Teachings of Ezra Taft Benson*, 404.

2. "The Issue: Starting out Right in Marriage," *Centered on Families*, 12.

Chapter 11—Romantic Love

1. *The Things of the Soul*. 1996, 106–7.

2. As told in Madsen, *Radiant Life*, 99–100.

3. "This I Believe," in *Brigham Young University 1991–92 Devotional and Fireside Speeches*, 1 Mar. 1992, 78.

4. *Eternal Love*, 4–5.

5. *You and Your Marriage*. 1960, 73.

6. "Marriage Is Honorable," in *Speeches of the Year: BYU Devotional and Ten-Stake Fireside*. 1974, 256.

7. *Writings of Parley Parker Pratt*, ed. Parker Pratt Robison. 1952, 53.

8. *Ensign*, July 1972, 112.

9. Reverend Billy Graham, as quoted in *Ensign*, May 1974, 7.

Chapter 12—Satan's Half-Truths about Romantic Love

1. *Things of the Soul*, 229.

2. In Conference Report, Oct. 1962, 56; or *Improvement Era*, Dec. 1962, 928.

3. *Faith Precedes the Miracle*. 1975, 154.

4. *Eternal Love*, 15.

5. "Marriage—The Great Mutual Improvement Association," *Brigham Young University Speeches of the Year* (6 Mar. 1961), 7–8.

6. As quoted by Christine Schultz in "Love," *US Airways Attache*, Feb. 1998, 50.

7. *Faith Precedes the Miracle*, 158.

8. *The Teachings of Spencer W. Kimball*, 281.

9. Ibid.

10. *A Faith to Live By*, 18.

11. *That All May Be Edified*. 1982, 38.

12. *Ensign*, Jan. 1973, 91.

13. *The Neal A. Maxwell Quote Book*, 1997, 205.

14. *The Teachings of Spencer W. Kimball*, 88.

15. *Ensign*, Jan. 1973, 131.

16. As quoted by Bruce C. and Marie K. Hafen, "Bridle All Your Passions," *Ensign*, Feb. 1994, 16.

Chapter 13—Friendship Love

1. "Priesthood and Partnerships," in AMCAP, 141.

2. As quoted by Elder Marlin K. Jensen, in *Ensign*, May 1999, 64.

3. *The Teachings of Spencer W. Kimball*, 310.

4. "Priesthood and Partnerships," in AMCAP, 139.

5. *Ensign*, June 1971, 56.

6. *Ensign*, May 1976, 62.

7. In Conference Report, Apr. 1968, 7–8; or *Improvement Era*, June 1968, 4.

8. "The Gospel and Romantic Love," *Ensign*, Oct. 1982, 67.

9. *Update*, 8.

10. In Conference Report, Apr. 1956, 9; or *Improvement Era*, June 1956, 396.

11. Brent A. Barlow, *Just for Newlyweds*. 1992, 74.

12. "The Issue: Starting out Right in Marriage," *Centered on Families*, 15–16.

13. Ibid.

14. As quoted by Jon Huntsman, "To Family Business and Humankind," *Exchange*, Magazine of the Marriott School of Management, Jan. 1999, 10.

15. *Ensign*, Nov. 1988, 23.

16. *Treasures of Life*, 60.

17. *Ensign*, May 1989, 26.

18. *Ensign*, Dec. 1971, 69.

19. *Ensign*, Nov. 1982, 60.

20. "Ten Keys to Successful Dating and Marriage Relationships," in *Brigham Young University 1981 Fireside and Devotional Speeches*. 1981, 70.

21. "Eternal Marriage," *Ensign*, Nov. 1984, 36–37; italics in original.

Chapter 14—Christlike Love

1. *History of the Church*, 5:23–24.

2. *Instructor*, May 1957, 130.

3. *The Teachings of Spencer W. Kimball*, 245.

4. In Conference Report, Apr. 1965, 71.

5. "Beauty for Ashes: The Atonement of Jesus Christ," *Ensign*, Apr. 1990, 7.

6. "And the Greatest of These Is Love," *Ensign*, Mar. 1984, 3.

7. *The Articles of Faith*. 1983, 438.

8. "Celestial Marriage," *Brigham Young University Speeches of the Year* (15 Nov. 1955), 2.

9. *Autobiography of Parley P. Pratt*. 1985, 259.

Chapter 15—The Secret to Successful Dating

1. *Ensign*, May 1997, 25.

2. *Ensign*, Oct. 1982, 67.

Chapter 16—What You Need to Know Should You Choose to Date Nonmembers

1. *The Teachings of Spencer W. Kimball*, 300.

2. *The Teachings of Gordon B. Hinckley*. 1997, 711.

3. "Marry within the Faith," *Church News*, 1 Feb. 1997, 2.

4. In Conference Report, Oct. 1956, 74.

5. *The Teachings of Spencer W. Kimball*, 301.

6. *Ensign*, Oct. 1979, 3.

7. Ibid.

8. *Journal of Discourses*, 11:118.

9. Pope, Essay on Man, *The Oxford Dictionary of Quotations*, epistle ii, lines 217–20.

10. *Ensign*, Oct. 1979, 4.

11. Ibid., 5–6.

12. *Ensign*, May 1991, 35.

Chapter 17—Ten Dimensions of an Eternal Relationship

1. *Ensign*, May 1988, 36–38.

2. "Views on Marriage Counseling and Making Church Member Marriages Work," in AMCAP. Vol. 16, no. 1, 99–100.

3. *One for the Money.* 1975, 1.

4. Ibid.

5. *You and Your Marriage*, 76.

6. *The Teachings of Ezra Taft Benson*, 384.

Chapter 18—Dealing with Differences

1. As quoted by Hartman, *Marriage—The Great Mutual Improvement Association*, 5.

2. "Marriage and Divorce," in *1976 Devotional Speeches of the Year.* 1977, 145–46.

3. *Ensign*, May 1974, 73.

4. *Your Agency: Handle with Care*, 111–12.

5. "Hinckleys to Note 60th Anniversary," 3.

6. *Your Agency: Handle with Care*, 111.

7. *Radiant Life*, 93.

8. *Dealing with Differences.* 1993, 10.

9. Adapted from *Marriage—The Great Mutual Improvement Association*, 10–12.

10. "Hinckleys to Note 60th Anniversary," 3.

11. Ibid.

Chapter 19—Breaking Up without Breaking Down

1. "Single Adults Counseled: Marriage Is a Righteous Goal," *Church News*, 5 Sept. 1992, 4.

2. "'Cast Not Away Therefore Your Confidence,'" in *Brigham Young University 1998–99 Speeches.* 1999, 4, 6; italics in original.

3. Adapted from M. Gawain Wells, "Breaking Up without Going to Pieces When Dating Doesn't End in Marriage," *Ensign*, June 1982, 58–61.

4. Ibid., 59.

5. *Go Forward with Faith: The Biography of Gordon B. Hinckley.* 1996, 423.

Chapter 20—Whom Shall You Marry?

1. In Conference Report, Apr. 1930, 82.

2. *The Teachings of Spencer W. Kimball*, 301.

3. *The Teachings of Gordon B. Hinckley*, 328.

4. "Agency or Inspiration—Which?" in *Speeches of the Year: BYU Devotional Addresses, 1972–1973.* 1973, 115–16.

5. *Radiant Life,* 101.

6. "John and Mary Beginning Life Together," *New Era,* June 1975, 7–8.

7. *Improvement Era,* July 1935, 460.

8. *Ensign,* May 1991, 35.

9. *The Teachings of Ezra Taft Benson,* 546.

Chapter 21—Temple Courtship

1. *Ensign,* May 1999, 26.

2. Ibid.

3. *That All May Be Edified,* 226–27.

Chapter 22—The Holy Temple

1. *Priesthood and Church Government.* 1939, 348.

2. "Ordinances of the Temple," *Church News,* 3 May 1997, 2.

3. *A Rational Theology.* 1926, 125.

4. *The House of the Lord.* 1976, 84.

5. *Mormon Doctrine.* 1989, 119.

6. Ibid., 118.

7. *The Holy Temple.* 1980, 144.

8. *The Things of the Soul.* 1996, 219–20.

Conclusion

1. *Journal of Discourses,* 2:90.

2. *The Teachings of Spencer W. Kimball,* 309.

About the Author

Robert K. McIntosh has been associated with the Church Educational System for twenty-eight years and is the director of the Santa Barbara (California) Institute of Religion. He has also worked as an independent business consultant. A graduate of Brigham Young University, he holds a master's degree in Church history and doctrine. Brother McIntosh has served in The Church of Jesus Christ of Latter-day Saints as a counselor in a stake presidency, as a member of the Church Melchizedek Priesthood writing committee, and as a counselor in the mission presidency of the California Ventura Mission. He and his wife, Susan, are the parents of five children and have nineteen grandchildren. They reside in Santa Barbara, California.